Foreign
Economic Relations
of the
European Community

Foreign Economic Relations of the European Community

The Impact of Spain and Portugal

Alfred Tovias

Lynne Rienner Publishers · Boulder & London

Published in the United States of America in 1990 by
Lynne Rienner Publishers, Inc.
1800 30th Street, Boulder, Colorado 80301

and in the United Kingdom by
Lynne Rienner Publishers, Inc.
3 Henrietta Street, Covent Garden, London WC2E 8LU

Library of Congress Cataloging-in-Publication Data
Tovias, Alfred.
  Foreign economic relations of the European Community: the impact
of Spain and Portugal / Alfred Tovias.
  Includes bibliographical references.
  ISBN 1-55587-175-5 (alk. paper)
  1. European Economic Community—Spain. 2. European Economic
Community—Portugal. 3. European Economic Community countries
—Foreign economic relations. I. Title.
HC241.25.S6T68 1990
337.4'0049—dc20   89-38557
                                                              CIP

British Cataloguing in Publication Data
A Cataloguing in Publication record for this book
is available from the British Library.

Printed and bound in the United States of America

The paper used in this publication meets the requirements
of the American National Standard for Permanence of
paper for Printed Library Materials Z39.48-1984.

Contents

List of Tables   vii
Acknowledgments   ix
List of Terms and Abbreviations   xi

1 Introduction   1

2 From Ten to Twelve: The EC After the Entry of   15
   Spain and Portugal

3 The Global Impact of New Member Countries on the   35
   Community's External Economic Policymaking

4 Economic Policies Toward Other Areas of the World   53

5 Summary and Conclusions   105

Notes   113
Bibliography   121
Index   131
About the Book and the Author   137

Tables

2.1 Geographical Distribution of Extra-EC-12 Exports by Percentage   18

2.2 Geographical Distribution of Extra-EC-12 Imports by Percentage   20

2.3 Index of Trade Vulnerability   24

2.4 Import Dependence Levels of Petroleum and Petroleum Products by Percentage   24

2.5 Import Dependence Levels of Gas and Gas Products by Percentage   26

2.6 Import and Export Levels of Dependence of Selected Third Countries by Percentage   30

2.7 Political Affiliation of Representatives to the European Parliament Before and After the Enlargement by Percentage   30

2.8 Political Affiliation of Representatives to the European Parliament After the First Two Direct Elections in Spain and Portugal by Percentage   32

3.1 Share of the EC's GNP and Population by Percentage   36

3.2 Share in EC Decisionmaking Power by Percentage   38

3.3 Official Spanish Development Assistance in 1984   44

3.4 Spain's ODA and Total Funds to Developing Countries as a Percentage of GNP   45

3.5 Distribution of Portuguese Economic Aid   47

4.1 Tourism to Spain from Non-EC Countries   55

4.2 Tourism to Portugal from Non-EC Countries   55

4.3 Number of Scheduled Airline Flights from Non-EC Countries per Week   56

4.4 Percentage of Scheduled Airline Flights per Week to the EC of All Flights from Non-EC Countries   57

4.5 Recipients of Spain's Direct Foreign Investment by Percentage   57

4.6 Foreign Investment in Spain as a Percentage of Total Foreign Investment   58

4.7 Spaniards Residing Outside Spain   59

4.8 Per Capita Income   68

Acknowledgments

Parts of the research for this book have been submitted at academic conferences, and the final text has benefited from the comments of colleagues who attended those conferences. In particular, I would like to thank George Yannopoulos of the Graduate School of European and International Studies of the University of Reading, Roy Ginsberg of Skidmore College, Alejandro Lorca of the Instituto de Economía y Geografía Aplicadas of the Consejo Superior de Investigaciones Científicas, Peter Praet of the Institut d'Etudes Européennes of the Université Libre de Bruxelles, Stephan Musto of the German Development Institute (Berlin), and Gianni Bonvicini of the Istituto d'Affari Internazionale (Rome).

I would like to thank Mrs. Lastenouse and her team of the Direction Générale de l'Information Universitaire at the EC Commission for their invaluable help setting up interviews with officials in Brussels. In this and related matters, the delegation of the EC Commission in Israel was also instrumental in helping me make contacts necessary to my research and I want to thank its staff.

Thanks are also due to the Leonard Davis Institute of International Relations of the Hebrew University for help in organizing and financing the 1987 Colloquium on "The Enlarged EC and the Mediterranean," which was the launching pad for the present book. I have received financial support for my research from the Jean Baugniet Fund of the Hebrew University and for preparation of the manuscript for the press both from the EC Commission and from the Davis Institute.

Although a goodly proportion of the most interesting information included was collected during personal interviews, not only in Brussels but also in Madrid and in Lisbon, many of those interviewed requested that they remain anonymous so they could feel free to express themselves more fully. I have therefore

listed all those with whom I spoke in my bibliography without
specific attribution in the text. I do, however, wish to thank them
all for their contributions. I would also like to express my
appreciation to the two anonymous readers, several of whose
comments have contributed to the final version of my text.
Finally, I want to thank Norma Schneider for her help in editing
the manuscript.

Alfred Tovias
July 1989

Terms and Abbreviations

Acquis Communautaire. The bylaws of the EC, or what each member must agree to adhere to upon joining

ACP. Former colonies in Africa, the Caribbean, and the Pacific Ocean

Arab World. Algeria, Bahrain, Democratic Yemen, Egypt, Iraq, Jordon, Kuwait, Lebanon, Libya, Mauritiania, Morocco, Oman, Qatar, Saudi Arabia, Sudan, Syria, Tunisia, United Arab Emirates, and Yemen

CAP. Common Agricultural Policy

CCT. Common Customs Tariff

Club of Paris. Ad hoc meeting (in Paris) of institutional lenders to deal with the case of a specific debtor country

COMPEX. Compensatory finance scheme launched in 1986 to cover below-normal export earnings of least developed countries that are not members to the Lome Convention

DAC. Development Assistance Committee, a subdivision of the OECD

EC. European Community

ECU. European Currency Unit (EC accounting unit and embryonic currency that comprises a basket of the currencies of the member countries)

EDF. European Development Fund

EFTA. Austria, Finland, Iceland, Norway, Sweden, and Switzerland

EIB. European Investment Bank

EMS. European Monetary System (set up in 1979)

EP. European Parliament

EPC. European Political Cooperation

ETA. Euzkadi Ta Azkatasuna, a Basque nationalist movement fighting for independence of the four Basque provinces by armed struggle against the Spanish state since the early 1960s

FAD. Spain's development aid fund

GATT. General Agreement on Tariffs and Trade

GDP. Gross Domestic Product

GMP. Global Mediterranean Policy

GNP. Gross National Product

GSP. Generalized System of Preferences

Lomé Convention. Multilateral agreement between the EC and ACP countries regarding tariffs, development aid, and stabilization of ACP export earnings

Mashrek. Egypt, Jordan, Lebanon, and Syria

Maghreb. Algeria, Morocco, and Tunisia

MFA. Multi-Fibre Arrangement

MPC. Mediterranean Policy Countries: Algeria, Cyprus, Egypt, Israel, Jordon, Lebanon, Malta, Morocco, Syria, and Tunisia

NIC. Newly Industrializing Country

ODA. Official Development Assistance

OECD. Organization for Economic Cooperation and Development

Reference Price System. A system under which a compensatory levy is applied when the selling price of a certain product exported to the EC falls below a given level, called the reference price

SEA. Single European Act

STABEX. Lomé Convention fund used to stabilize the export earnings of ACP countries from agricultural commodities

UNCTAD. United Nations Conference on Trade and Development

1

Introduction

The entry of Spain and Portugal into the European Community
(EC) on January 1, 1986 was the culmination of drawn out
negotiations that lasted for almost ten years. These two Southern
European countries, both of which have achieved a transition
from dictatorship to democracy with considerable success, joined
the EC at a time when—despite the countless crises that are bound
to arise in any such enterprise—there is no doubt that the
Community is and will remain a given in contemporary
international relations.

The Customs Union, the Common Agricultural Policy (CAP),
the European Monetary System (EMS), and the framework for
European Political Cooperation (EPC) appear to be solid pillars of
the European construct. The European Parliament (EP), too, is
slowly but surely increasing its legitimacy and presence in the
continent's public life; and the amendments of the Treaty of
Rome, in the form of the Single European Act (SEA), ratified by
every EC member in early 1987, should act to improve the
decisionmaking process at the Council of Ministers level.
Moreover, now that new voting rules related to a real internal
market have been included in the SEA, the prospect of achieving
that goal by 1992 appears realistic. Thus, it seems that the
European Community of the Twelve is set for a new takeoff and
is viewed by the outside world as being in full swing.

One might, of course, doubt the likelihood of future internal
cohesion in a group comprised of twelve Western European
countries, each of which has very different political traditions
and backgrounds. In this context, adding two more countries
would seem, a priori, to make already complicated interactions
even more difficult. On the other hand, one might look at the
bright side and realize that the two newest member states share a
highly positive attitude toward the European idea, which was
certainly not the case when lukewarm Britain and Denmark

1

joined, almost two decades ago. Thus, although quantitatively speaking the EC might be more difficult to manage because reaching decisions will now be more cumbersome, the cooperative mood in regard to European integration matters that so far seems to prevail in Spain and Portugal should partially compensate for this.[1] Therefore, assuming that internal cohesion does not basically change, and/or that the European Community does not become paralyzed, it appears that the new European Community of the Twelve looks quite different from the previous one in that:

1. It is much more "Mediterranean."
2. It has more features in common with newly industrializing economies such as Israel, and fewer features in common with highly developed countries such as Sweden and Switzerland.
3. It includes two ex-colonial powers, which, like France and the United Kingdom, make a pretense of having special responsibilities in different areas of the world.
4. It will now become an agricultural superpower.
5. It is now more culturally diverse.
6. Marine-, coastal-, seabed-, and fishing-related resources have increased significantly because of the Peninsula's Atlantic coast.

The shock to different areas of the world of the Southern Enlargement of the Community has already been widely analyzed,[2] with different scholars more or less in agreement on the extent to which specific third (nonmember) countries will be affected by the accession of Spain and Portugal. I shall therefore draw upon previous work when necessary, rather than reanalyzing the subject. Nor do I deal with the specifics of negotiations between the EC and third countries with regard to compensating the latter (either in the context of the General Agreement on Tariffs and Trade (GATT) or elsewhere) for any negative impact on their exports to the Community. In this respect, it can be said not only that the once-and-for-all negative impact of the Enlargement will eventually be absorbed and neutralized, but—independently of this—that new EC policies will have to be developed to deal with different geographic regions as a consequence of the structural change in the Community itself. Moreover, the change in the dimension and geographic size of the EC will no doubt have a significant impact on the Community's relations with the outside world. It is the investigation of these closely linked aspects of the Enlargement of the EC to include Spain and Portugal that is the true aim of the book.

While the impact of the Southern Enlargement on future intra-Community (e.g., agricultural) policies has been abundantly studied, this is not the case with respect to how the enlarged EC's new power will affect future foreign economic relations. Indeed, a distinctive feature of my presentation is that it proposes a broad macroview of the direction that future EC foreign economic policies will take. Moreover, the text incorporates many new items that previous studies on the Community's foreign relations could not take into account before the Iberian Enlargement, with all of its special features. In this context, for example, reference can be made to *The External Economic Policy of the Enlarged Community*, the book issued after the 1972 Bruges Week, organized by the College of Europe. For, when we consult the table of contents of that work,[3] we can see that, while no space was devoted to Latin America, two chapters tackled relations with Commonwealth countries, and—because the United Kingdom was and still is a major power—several chapters dealt with East-West relations. In contrast, the present work aims at breaking new ground, in line with the new situation created by the entry of Spain and Portugal into the Community.

The European Community's Pyramid of Influence

As stressed by numerous authors,[4] the EC now applies a regionalist philosophy to its common external trade policy, as opposed to the multilateral approach favored by the GATT. During the first decade of its existence, whenever the Community was approached by any country that wanted to receive special treatment, it always stressed that its obligations in GATT made this impossible.[5] Former colonies—including Maghreb countries—were, however, treated differently. After all, preferential agreements between colonies and their metropolis that had been concluded before January 1, 1948 (when GATT went into effect) had been accepted under Article 1, Paragraph 2 of the General Agreement (notwithstanding the clause of unconditional most-favored-nation treatment contained in Paragraph 1 of the same Article).

The assumption of former colonial responsibilities in the trade field by the original Community of the Six (France, West Germany, Italy, and Benelux countries) was not viewed as a violation of the spirit of GATT; and the same good conscience dominated Eurocrat thinking when referring to associated countries in the southern periphery of the Community. Association agreements signed with Greece, Turkey, Malta, and Cyprus under Article 238 of the Treaty of Rome were nothing more than the EC's interpretation of the "interim agreements leading to customs unions or free trade areas" provided for in Article 24 of the GATT. These latter four countries, a part of Europe not yet able to assume the obligations of membership because of their economic backwardness, had to be linked to the EC by some form of interim agreement leading to membership. Nor was the EC's 1971 adoption of its own Generalized System of Preferences (GSP) scheme in favor of exports from developing countries a signal indicating distaste toward the multilateral approach of GATT. The principle of conceding generalized preference to Third World countries had been accepted in 1969 by all trade partners in the Organization for Economic Co-operation and Development (OECD) except for the United States.

The EFTA and ACP Countries

In my opinion, the drifting away from the GATT approach was an outcome of the First Enlargement of the EC to include Britain in 1973 (although there had been signs of that drift as early as 1970 when the EC concluded partial preferential agreements with Spain and Israel). This was the first time that the Community decided to help solve problems of fellow OECD developed countries deriving from the Enlargement of the area of economic integration *by adopting a regional approach*. The decision was to compensate European Free Trade Association (EFTA) countries not under GATT Article 24, Paragraph 6, but rather to propose that affected countries conclude individual free-trade agreements with the Community. Surprisingly, this procedure did not provoke an uproar in the United States.

The probable reason for the Community's change of heart was the realization that a regional approach to commercial policy, when applied by a huge trade bloc such as the Nine (the original Six, plus Britain, Denmark, and Ireland), would maximize the Community's influence on those areas of the world that were highly dependent on trade with the EC. Why, they reasoned, spread influence thinly over more than 160 countries in the system, when most of these countries have few trade or political links with the Community and are outside its orbit? Since influence is gained by distribution of privileges, they thought, the latter was an essential element in their strategy. In this regard, I take issue with previous work that stresses the means ("conferring privilege") and does not focus on the aim of the whole exercise: to exert influence. Hindsight shows us that the EC's free trade agreements with seven individual EFTA countries (Switzerland, Austria, Sweden, Finland, Iceland, Norway, and Portugal) were instrumental in shaping its order of regional priorities in accordance with the degree of influence it could exert in each case: The higher the degree of trade dependence of the nonmember, and the lower its strategic importance for a superpower, the more substantial the EC's influence. Not surprisingly, EFTA countries were at the top of the pyramid, almost on a par with former colonies in Africa, the Caribbean, and the Pacific Ocean (ACP countries), sixty-six of which are signatories to the last of three five-year-long multilateral treaties institutionalizing the links of ACP countries with the EC since 1975. Since these treaties were signed in Lomé, the capital of Togo, they are known as the Lomé Conventions. A new treaty between the EC and ACP countries, the fourth of a series, is currently being negotiated to replace what is popularly known as Lomé III, an agreement that expires in February 1990.

The Mediterranean Countries

The Mediterranean was another matter altogether. While in some cases the trade dependence on the EC of the countries in the area was as high as that of ACP or EFTA countries, this was not always the case—particularly for Eastern Mediterranean countries such as Egypt, Israel, and Syria. Moreover, the involvement in the region's economies of the United States and the USSR through economic and military aid designed to foster their own power in the area, was overriding. Correspondingly, the Global Mediterranean Policy (GMP) of the EC, launched in 1972, was placed further down the ladder of importance. This policy consisted of a series of cooperation agreements with Maghreb (Morocco, Algeria, and Tunisia) and Mashrek (Egypt, Lebanon, Syria, and Jordan) countries, together with a free trade agreement for industrial products with Israel. The agreement with Israel was based on full reciprocity, while the other agreements provided only for free access of the industrial exports of the Mediterranean partner into the European Community and partial tariff reductions for agricultural imports.

GSP, GATT, and Some Eastern European Countries

The three remaining layers of the EC influence pyramid—GSP countries, GATT countries, and some Eastern European countries—must be considered to have been placed in the ranking by the EC involuntarily. The GSP was not an EC invention, but rather an idea imposed from above. Nor is GATT membership decided by the European Community; since EC members were all GATT Contracting Parties before joining the Community, the EC must confer at least GATT treatment to fellow Contracting Parties. The last layer consists of countries in Eastern Europe that do not belong to GATT and to which, for obvious reasons, the Community had no hope whatsoever of extending its influence until very recently.

The Third Enlargement of the European Community

The First Enlargement of the Community—from six to nine members—took place on January 1, 1973, when Britain, Denmark, and Ireland joined what was then called the Six. Greece joined the Nine on January 1, 1981, an event that some scholars term the Second Enlargement, while others reserve this expression for the accession of Spain, Portugal, and Greece. Those who prefer the latter definition frequently refer to the EC's Northern Enlargement of 1973, as opposed to its Southern Enlargement, when Greece joined in 1981, followed by the entry of Spain and Portugal in 1986. Since the latter two joined together, and since it now appears that other Southern European countries (e.g., Turkey, Malta, and Cyprus) may join in a number of years, it seems preferable to use the term Third Enlargement when speaking of the Iberian countries' entry into the EC. It is particularly appropriate to do so in this book, which does not in any case deal with Greece's entry. For, not only did that occur much sooner than the entry of Spain and Portugal, but the circumstances of Greece's joining were quite different, because, e.g., the latter had been associated with the EC since 1962, and had suffered an authoritarian regime for "only" seven years, not the forty- and fifty-year dictatorships that had prevailed in Spain and Portugal, respectively, until the mid-1970s.

The treaty providing for the accession of Spain and Portugal into the European Community was signed on June 12, 1985. As demonstrated by the fact that the official text of the treaty runs to three volumes,[6] "Operation Enlargement to Spain and Portugal" was complex. Of course, the actual accession in 1986 did not take place in a vacuum; there were already important institutional links between the parties. Schematically speaking, the most relevant parametric changes that accompanied the entry of Spain and Portugal into the Community—from the perspective of nonmember countries[7]—are listed below:

Agricultural and Industrial Trade

1. The two countries are adjusting their customs duties progressively to the level of the EC's Common Customs Tariff (CCT), and will adopt it completely by January 1, 1993 (with the exception of some products for which the deadline is advanced by several years). This step invariably implies a reduction in tariff protection levels on non-EC countries' industrial exports, although not for agricultural commodities such as coffee. (It should be noted that the Canary Islands and Ceuta and Melilla are excluded from the Customs Union.)

Agricultural Trade

1. Spain and Portugal will obtain free access to the EC for their agricultural products by 1996, thereby improving their previous status of preferred Mediterranean and EFTA country, respectively, which entailed very few tariff reductions.

2. The European Community will obtain free access into the new members' agricultural markets for most products by 1996 and for a minority of products, such as beef and veal, by 1993.

3. The new members will benefit progressively from all the advantages of the CAP (e.g., they will obtain export refunds, receive guaranteed prices, and so on) until their full integration in 1996. After a while, they will also have to respect such common disciplines as corresponsibility prices, some production restraints and quality requirements, as well as to apply the principle of Community preference and common agricultural prices. (The Canary Islands and Ceuta and Melilla will not apply the CAP.)

4. Portugal and Spain will progressively liberalize their mutual trade in agricultural products and will reach free trade by 1990.

5. Trade between the new members and the EC will be subject to a seven-year transition period for most fish products, except for a number of sensitive species, for which the transition period ends in 1996.

Industrial Trade

1. According to the Treaty of Accession, Spain and Portugal, on the one hand, and the EC on the other must progressively increase their margins of preference on mutual industrial trade to 100%, attaining a level of free trade in industrial goods by 1993. In fact, and in view of the tremendous Spanish trade deficit with the EC since 1986, the Community decided in early 1989 to grant duty-free access into the EC to Spanish industrial exports already by July 1, 1989. (This change has much more significance for Spain than for Portugal, which has had free access to the EC—except for textile trade—since before 1986, and by implementation of the 1972 Free Trade Agreement offered the EC a wider access to its market than did Spain, which has been linked to the EC since 1970 by a partial preferential agreement.) Here, it must be noted too that the Community will have to suppress all surveillance measures on Spain's textile exports to EC countries by 1990.

2. Portugal and Spain will progressively liberalize their mutual trade in industrial products, reaching free trade by 1990.

Trade Relations with Third Countries

1. According to a series of protocols attached to the Treaty of Accession, the new members shall obtain tariff-free access for their industrial exports and preferential status for their agricultural exports in the EFTA and Israeli market by 1993. In fact, EFTA decided to grant Spanish industrial exports duty-free access already by July 1, 1989, following a similar decision made by the EC (see *Industrial trade* 1. above). Moreover, Cyprus, Malta, and Turkey will give Spain and Portugal preferences on their exports. This change also has much more significance for Spain than for Portugal, because as one of its original members the latter benefited from free access to EFTA (except for textile

trade) even before 1986, whereas Spain only received partial preferences through an agreement concluded in 1979.

2. By 1993 all Mediterranean nonmembers (except for Albania and Libya) and ACP countries will have free access into the Spanish and Portuguese industrial markets without any limitations on their exports. GSP countries will obtain tariff-free treatment in these markets, but with limitations. The alignment of tariffs on the EC's preferential rate is being made progressively, from March 1, 1986, through January 1, 1993—for manufactured goods and fish products—and through January 1, 1996—for agricultural exports. Here observe that the proportional tariff reduction for imports originating from these countries is much larger than for those from the EC or EFTA, because the starting tariff applied by Spain and Portugal was already lower in the latter case.

3. Agricultural exports from ACP countries will have obtained complete free access into Iberian markets by the end of the transition period. Moreover the latter's agricultural imports originating in Mediterranean countries will benefit from partial tariff preferences on a much wider scale than under the GSP scheme.

4. The new members must adopt the EC textile agreements as well as agreements dealing with manioc, sheep, and lamb meat with several developing countries.

5. Upon expiry, fishing agreements between Spain or Portugal and third countries will be replaced by Community agreements with these countries.

6. Spain has had to withdraw from a scheme of trade preferences among developing countries that was concluded in 1971.

7. Spain has included several unilateral declarations concerning relations with Latin America in the Annexes of its Treaty of Accession, but these do not impose any obligation on the parties to the Treaty per se.

8. As an outcome of pressure exerted by Mediterranean nonmember countries, alarmed by the prospects deriving from items 1 and 3 on agricultural trade mentioned above, the EC has added new protocols to the agreements concluded with nonmembers in the mid-1970s. As in the case of Spain, these new protocols provide for the progressive elimination of customs duties on traditional quantities of fruits and vegetables exported to the European Community by these third Mediterranean countries. As a quid pro quo, the Canary Islands and Ceuta and Melilla will be accorded the same treatment received by other

Mediterranean countries under these new additional protocols. These therefore must be seen as part of "Operation Enlargement."

As stated above, this book does not deal with the implications for third countries of the parametric changes described.[8] Of course Spain, Portugal, and the Community will take into account the static and dynamic effects of the Enlargement when designing their foreign policies.

The Relationship Among Enlargement, Deepening, and Protectionism

Most experts agree that the fear that a further Enlargement would hopelessly tie up the decisionmaking mechanisms of the European Community has pushed EC heads of state to accept institutional reform. There is no doubt that the Single European Act (SEA), which has been ratified by all EC member parliaments, was at least partly a consequence of the entry of Spain and Portugal into the Community. The SEA extends weighted majority voting beyond what had been the practice in the Community for more than two decades. Moreover, in the early 1980s, Northern European countries, such as Britain, Denmark, and the Netherlands, realized that there was not much profit to be reaped by their exporters from the new Enlargement (as compared with the benefits received by France, Italy, or West Germany). It was time then for the Community to adopt as its own some of the Northern bloc's suggestions, including one suggestion that was particularly attractive to their exporters: the elimination of nontariff barriers on intra-Community high-tech and service exports.

According to this view, the 1985 Commission proposals for the completion of the Internal Market by 1992, which was enthusiastically supported by Northern European countries, must also be seen as an indirect outcome of the Southern European countries' entry into the EC. This is not a new phenomenon: every time that an Enlargement was being negotiated, there were voices in the Community for deepening the integration process. However, both the Enlargement and the completion of the Internal Market by 1992 will imply more specialization over a wider area than previously. If this tendency is not counteracted, economists and politicians expect this will lead to internal

tension between the members of the Community of the Twelve.[9] ✗
This is the baseline, as far as the subject of this book is
concerned.

The reason for this is simply that there are not many political
options to diffuse friction among members. Of course, one way
out of this dilemma would be to paralyze the integration process.
Another would be internal redistribution and/or adjustment. A
third option would be *more protectionism*—which is the danger as
perceived from the periphery of the Community. Such increased
protectionism could take the form of erosion or impairment of
former privileges (e.g., the inclusion of more horticultural
products in the CAP). But increased protectionism presents two
drawbacks for the European Community: (1) a loss of influence
over preferred trade partners, and (2) a possible destabilization of
third country political regimes.

A second kind of response by the Community would be to
impose new barriers on those countries that never had privileged
status (e.g., the United States, Canada, and Eastern Europe) or
that were less privileged (e.g., GSP countries). Here, the main
risk would be retaliation. A third possibility—combining the last
two strategies—would carry the risk that new alliances might be
formed between countries that were privileged and those that
were not.

A priori, Spain and Portugal—as opposed to Britain and
Denmark (and a left-wing government in Greece)—would not be
keen on paralyzing the integration process. But the adjustment
option depends essentially on how large a majority the present
government has and how soon the next elections are.

In this respect, there are contradicting trends. On the one
hand, the stability of the present majorities in the Spanish Cortes
and the Portuguese Parliament indicates a wide margin of
maneuver for the governments of these two countries to impose
adjustment. On the other hand, the amount of adjustment that
must be absorbed by the Spanish and Portuguese public in a
matter of ten years seems significant (Enlargement, Internal
Market, Uruguay Round, etc.). Thus, the governments might be
tempted to prolong adjustment. Moreover, a Socialist government in Spain might even favor redistribution/solidarity,
especially if Spain is at the receiving end, although it is less
clear what would happen if she were at the giving end (e.g., in the
form of more defense expenditures for the joint defense of the
West). Since adjustment cum redistribution has these possible
limitations, the new members may decide anyway to favor

European neomercantilism. This is where their foreign policy regional priorities and regional economic interests enter the picture.

According to the above scheme, Spain and Portugal will try to target increased EC protectionism in the direction of nonmember countries wherever their own economic/security assets or their "capital of sympathy" are either not at stake or may not be affected negatively by new protectionist measures. Conversely, they will try to erode privileges previously conceded to countries where loss of influence by the EC leaves Spain or Portugal indifferent. In the same vein, the new members will push the EC system to increase barriers on imports originating in countries that either cannot retaliate directly against Spain or Portugal, or that have tremendous bilateral trade surpluses with the two new members. Of course, to this list may be added countries the Iberians want to punish for some reason.

As will be shown in the coming chapters, both Spain and Portugal seem to be conforming to this model of behavior.

Plan of the Book

In Chapter 2, the structural changes of the European Community—when it grew from Ten to Twelve—that may affect its relations with nonmembers are reviewed. The question asked in this chapter is: what changes has this caused in the profile of the EC in regard to the Community's different areas of activity? Of interest here are changes in the levels of trade and energy dependence on different areas of the world. The new image of the European Community in the world, as well as the trade dependence of third countries on the enlarged EC are also discussed. Finally, changes in the political map of the European Parliament are briefly examined.

Chapter 3 provides an analysis of the global impact of the Spanish and Portuguese governments in the EC decisionmaking process, with the focus on past and present Spanish and Portuguese economic policies. It takes into account that, at present, their economic policies are strongly influenced by the need to integrate into the European Community fully after a transition period. Also dealt with in this section is the fact that countries which already belonged to the EC must also adjust to the economic impact made by the newcomers, and that, the policies of both old and new members vis-a-vis external EC relations will be strongly influenced by what goes on within the EC itself as a result of Enlargement. An analysis of all these interconnected issues allows for an evaluation of the relative weight of foreign and domestic affairs in the post-enlargement Community. But before engaging in this analysis, we assess the weight of the new entrants and of the older Mediterranean members of the EC in terms of different economic, demographic, and political variables.

In Chapter 4, the focus is placed on the very specific issue of the interests of Spain and Portugal in relation to different EC foreign economic policies. We shall not, of course, consider all the countries of the world, but will restrict ourselves to those areas for which the entry of Spain and Portugal may a priori make a difference. This obviously includes Latin America and the Mediterranean. However, as EC policies in a number of other geographic areas may also be affected by the new members' entry, we have chosen for selective study the Euro-Arab dialogue and EC relations with ACP and EFTA countries as well as with the United States. Once we know something about the position of the two new entrants on these policies, the obvious question to be answered is: will Spanish and Portuguese views on the various issues at stake coincide or diverge sharply?

In Chapter 5, comprising a summary and some conclusions, the question of whether there will be a new internal balance in the new Community due to differences between the foreign policies of its old and new members is addressed. We shall also take up the question of whether a Southern European lobby will emerge, and if so, what effect it will have on external EC policies.

A note of caution is warranted before concluding these remarks on the book's contents: The focus herein is on EC economic—and not political—relations with different regions of the world. However, since the distinction between the two levels is often difficult to make (e.g., in relation to the Euro-Arab dialogue), the political dimension cannot be altogether ignored.

2

From Ten to Twelve: The EC After the Entry of Spain and Portugal

A Panoramic View

The entry of Spain and Portugal into the EC in 1986 has had a significant impact on its size or dimension in some domains. It is these areas of significance that must be the object of attention here, because they may alter the weight and image of the Community in the world. The areas in which the change is substantial do not depend on the discretion of the new or old member states, but can be described quantitatively:[10]

1. The EC's agricultural land increased by 34.7%, whereas agricultural production and employment increased by 12% and 36.3%, respectively. According to the U.S. Department of Agriculture, in 1986 the EC became the world's leading exporter of agricultural products, ahead of the United States. This is partly a reflection of the inclusion of Spain and Portugal. Moreover the Community's territory increased by 36%, so that it is now one-quarter the size of the United States instead of one sixth. Beyond its agricultural implications, this change has strategic value as well.

2. The population of the EC increased by 18%, from 273 to 322 million people. The population of the Community is now 38% larger than that of the United States instead of 23% larger. The respective percentages in relation to Japan, another trade superpower, are 168% and 128%. This increase indicates a higher absorption capacity and makes the EC more attractive for direct investments.

3. The total coastal length increased by 12%, which is of importance in mining, tourism, merchant navy, and fishing. Given the double character of the Peninsula as an Atlantic- and Mediterranean-bordering region, the respective weight of the two

rims in the EC's total coastal length has not changed, practically speaking.

4. The geographical center of gravity of the Community moved south. A convenient indicator, using demographic data, is the increased weight of the Mediterranean countries in the European Parliament, from 35.9% to 52.12%; in the Commission, from 29.4% to 47.1%; and in the Council of Ministers, from 32.9% to 50%.[11]

5. The demographic weight of countries whose most-used language is English diminished from 22% to 18%.

6. The weight of the EC countries that are also NATO members increased slightly, as has their weight in the Atlantic Alliance.[12]

7. The per capita GNP of the EC decreased by 8.5%, from $9852 to $9017. While Belgium previously represented the average Community standard of living ($9510), this country is now clearly in the more affluent group (together with Denmark, France, Germany, The Netherlands, and Luxembourg). On the other hand, there is a distinguishable group of four countries— namely Spain, Ireland, Greece, and Portugal—whose per capita GNP is much below average. Now the UK represents the average community standard of living ($9000).

8. The EC's trade dependence on different areas of the world has changed marginally. This point is a key variable in explaining possible changes in the sensitivity of the Community towards particular regions or continents, and is discussed in detail below.

9. Regarding crude oil imports, the EC's outside dependence levels have not changed vis-a-vis Arab countries, but have increased markedly in relation to the Middle East. Interestingly, these levels decreased in relation to OPEC.

EC Trade Dependence on Different Areas of the World

Tables 2.1 and 2.2 give calculations using OECD data on the distribution of trade by Spain, Portugal, and the EC with the "outside world" for 1976, 1980, and 1984. "Outside world" refers to the world less the two other European trade partners mentioned (e.g., Portugal and the Ten, in the case of Spain).

Five different areas have been selected for particular study: Mediterranean countries that are not members of the EC; Latin America, including Mexico and Central America; the United

States; the EFTA countries, not including Portugal; and ACP countries. All other non-EC countries are included under "Others."

Because OECD statistics include a special grouping called Non-OECD Mid East, it has been shown separately, given the relative vulnerability of European countries to this area in the past.

The following analysis is based on material in Table 2.1.

Time-Series Analysis

Spain. By the end of 1984, Mediterranean countries replaced Latin America as the most important area of destination for Spanish exports. In 1984, the United States and Mediterranean countries represented more than 40% of the Spanish exports not directed to the Community. The share of EFTA and ACP countries were quite small throughout the period.

Portugal. The United States and the EFTA countries were Portugal's principal extra-Community markets throughout the period, accounting for more than 45% of the total. But within this developed country category, the United States gained weight to the detriment of the EFTA countries. When focusing on developing countries, ACP and Mediterranean countries increased their weight over Latin America.

EC10. For the Ten, the EFTA and Mediterranean countries together accounted for more than one-third of extra-EC exports. The United States was also an important market. The ACP and Latin American markets were of secondary importance.

Cross-Sectional Analysis

Comparing Spain with Portugal—Spain appears to have concentrated on penetrating Mediterranean and Latin American markets, while Portugal developed its sales in the EFTA and ACP countries. Both countries placed equal emphasis on cultivating the U.S. market, an area important to both of them.

Comparing Spain to the Ten—both the Mediterranean and Latin American markets have a much higher profile in Spain's exports than in those of the Ten, while the reverse holds for EFTA markets. There is no sharp divergence in regard to the U.S. and ACP markets.

Table 2.1
Geographical Distribution of Extra-EC-12 Exports by Percentage

	Spain			Portugal			EC-10			EC-12		
	1976	1980	1984	1976	1980	1984	1976	1980	1984	1976	1980	1984
Mediterranean Countries	17.19	20.84	21.55	6.58	5.89	9.67	12.60	12.19	11.72	12.71	12.44	12.12
(Med. Policy countries)	(11.70)	(14.77)	(15.72)	(4.38)	(4.28)	(7.53)	(6.92)	(7.07)	(7.24)	(7.05)	(7.31)	(7.60)
Latin America	19.14	21.66	11.30	5.11	6.19	2.36	6.91	6.64	5.12	7.25	7.13	5.36
United States	19.88	11.41	19.34	14.50	13.64	23.19	12.11	12.02	20.64	12.35	12.01	20.60
EFTA[a]	9.29	8.27	7.46	34.51	33.23	27.52	23.44	24.61	21.89	23.09	24.13	21.34
ACP	5.68	7.06	6.17	9.68	15.97	14.20	5.09	7.31	4.94	5.13	7.36	5.00
Others	28.82	30.76	34.18	29.62	25.08	23.06	39.85	37.23	35.69	39.47	36.93	35.58
TOTALS	100.00	100.00	100.00	100.00	100.00	100.00	100.00	100.00	100.00	100.00	100.00	100.00
Non-OECD Mid East	8.35	14.30	13.09	3.02	4.51	6.08	11.08	10.99	12.33	11.66	11.06	12.22

Source: OECD Foreign Trade by Commodities, various years.
[a]Not including Portugal

Comparing Portugal to the Ten—both EFTA and ACP markets had a much higher profile in Portugal's exports than in that of the Ten, while the reverse holds for Mediterranean markets. There was no sharp divergence in regard to the U.S. and Latin American markets.

The comparison between the Ten and the Twelve—which is especially relevant for our purpose—shows: (1) the importance of Mediterranean countries as a destination for EC exports increases marginally, and (2) the same applies for Latin America, while (3) the weight of the U.S. remains the same, (4) the importance of EFTA markets decreases marginally, and (5) the share of ACP in EC exports remains stable.

The insignificant change in EC's export dependence levels on different regions is partly due to the fact that Portugal and Spain's opposing levels of export dependence cancel each other out in the EC-12: EFTA is much more important for Portugal than for Spain, while the reverse is true regarding Mediterranean countries. This is valid independently of the fact that Spain carries more weight than Portugal in the construction of the EC-12 index. Moreover, when we focus on 1976 instead of 1984 we get the same results, except for a marginal increase of the EC index of dependence on the United States, showing that while Spain was much more dependent on the U.S. market than on the EC-10 or Portugal in 1976, the reverse was true eight years later.

Time-Series Analysis

The following analysis is based on material in Table 2.2

Spain. Between 1976 and 1984 developing countries in the Mediterranean Basin, Africa, and Latin America raised their total share of imports to Spain from 22.16% to 38.52%. Spanish imports from EFTA and the United States, on the other hand, dropped from 28.57% to 22.84%. Nevertheless, the United States and Latin America remained Spain's principal extra-EC suppliers, followed by Mediterranean countries.

Portugal. Latin America, ACP countries, and the United States markedly increased their profile in the Portuguese market, to the great detriment of the EFTA countries. At the end of the period, the United States was by far Portugal's principal extra-EC supplier, followed by Latin America, ACP, and the EFTA countries.

Table 2.2
Geographical Distribution of Extra-EC-12 Imports by Percentage

	Spain			Portugal			EC-10			EC-12		
	1976	1980	1984	1976	1980	1984	1976	1980	1984	1976	1980	1984
Mediterranean Countries	8.02	10.02	11.76	5.02	3.44	6.57	8.07	8.05	10.24	8.03	8.11	10.28
(Med. Policy countries)	(2.91)	(4.32)	(5.66)	(2.06)	(2.99)	(4.78)	(3.71)	(4.22)	(5.50)	(3.65)	(4.20)	(5.53)
Latin America	10.64	15.19	17.98	8.46	9.15	12.59	6.23	6.14	7.20	6.54	6.72	8.02
United States	21.39	18.91	17.19	18.24	19.88	23.62	16.25	16.04	16.91	16.60	16.26	17.03
EFTA[a]	7.18	5.16	5.65	19.44	13.82	9.00	15.92	16.39	20.02	15.41	15.68	18.98
ACP	3.50	5.34	8.78	7.31	7.59	10.94	5.18	6.83	6.71	5.1	6.75	6.90
Others	49.27	45.38	38.64	41.53	46.12	37.28	48.35	46.55	38.92	52.91	46.48	38.79
TOTALS	100.00	100.00	100.00	100.00	100.00	100.00	100.00	100.00	100.00	100.00	100.00	100.00
Non-OECD Mid East	31.46	31.88	23.16	20.31	30.26	24.55	21.30	18.18	9.09	21.93	19.16	10.18

Source: OECD Foreign Trade by Commodities, various years.
[a]Not including Portugal

EC-10. During the entire period, the EFTA countries and the United States accounted for more than one-third of extra-area imports, with the Mediterranean countries following. ACP and Latin American suppliers were of secondary importance.

From the above, it becomes clear that:

- For Spain: the Mediterranean countries were more important as markets than as suppliers, while the reverse held true for Latin America. For other countries, there were few differences between their status as a supplier or as a market.
- For Portugal: The EFTA, ACP, and Mediterranean countries were much more important as markets than as suppliers, while the reverse held true for Latin America.
- For the EC-10: The EFTA countries and the United States were much more important as markets than as suppliers; while the reverse held for Latin America, the differences were not as substantial as for Spain or Portugal.

Cross-Sectional Analysis

Comparing Spain with Portugal. Spain imported more than Portugal from Latin America and the Mediterranean, while the reverse was true for the United States, EFTA, and ACP countries. However, countries covered by the Mediterranean Policy had the same importance for both Spain and Portugal as suppliers.

Comparing Spain to the EC-10. The heavy reliance of the EC-10 on EFTA suppliers contrasted with the large role of Latin American imports on Spain. For the rest, there were no major differences.

Comparing Portugal to the EC-10. Portugal imported more from Latin America, the United States, and ACP countries and less from EFTA and Mediterranean countries than the Ten.

Comparing the EC-10 with the EC-12. There are quite a few differences between import and export dependence: (1) the weight of Mediterranean (and Mediterranean Policy) countries did not change, (2) Latin America's share of total imports into the Community rose substantially, (3) the share of U.S. originating imports increased marginally, (4) the importance of EFTA-originating imports diminished substantially, and (5) the ACP's share did not change.

Both Portugal and Spain relied heavily on Latin American suppliers in comparison to the old Community, which explains the substantial change in EC dependence on Latin America. Thus, contrary to what happened in the area of exports, Portugal and Spain are on the same side of the import divide—both countries rely less on EFTA suppliers than the EC's average, which explains the reduction in EC import dependence on EFTA. This conclusion would have been less striking had the comparison been made in 1976, when Portugal relied more heavily on EFTA and less so on Latin American suppliers.

Turning to the last line of Tables 2.1 and 2.2, which deals with the Non OECD Mid East, we see that in 1984 Spain's export dependence levels were similar to those of the Ten, but those of Portugal were only half as high. Given Portugal's small weight in total EC trade flows, it is not surprising that export dependence levels do not change when we consider the EC at Twelve rather than at Ten.

Regarding the 1984 import dependence levels, the picture is quite different, because in relative terms Spain and Portugal imported more than twice as much as the Ten from the non-OECD Middle East. Hence, import dependence levels change by one full percentage point when Spain and Portugal are included in the calculations.

In conclusion, it seems that the incorporation of the Iberian Peninsula into the European Community would not have made a radical difference in the 1976, 1980, or 1984 export dependence levels of any of the areas selected for study. However, when we focus on import dependence levels, the situation is different because—at least in 1980 and 1984—a European Community that included Spain and Portugal would have relied more heavily on Middle East and Latin American supplies than an EC without them. The exact reverse would be the case in relation to EFTA.

This does not necessarily imply that increased import dependence on the Middle East or Latin America and less reliance on EFTA suppliers is to be expected in the future. The adoption by Spain and Portugal of the "acquis communautaire"—what each member must agree to adhere to upon joining the EC—in relation to EFTA, Mediterranean, and ACP countries may change the geographical distribution of Spanish and Portuguese extra-Community trade drastically, so that their external trade patterns will eventually converge with those of the EC. However, the same figures may also point to a slightly different sensitivity of the two acceding countries, when compared to the old EC, regarding Latin America and the Middle East. This might push them to strive for a different ordering of priorities in dealing with EC external economic policies.

To illustrate this point, in Table 2.3 we have taken the 1984 figures for export and import dependence levels on different areas of the world and aggregated them to show dependence levels ordered according to the present EC "pyramid of privilege." This composite figure can be interpreted as an index of trade vulnerability to different zones of the world. (Latin America and the Middle East have been included at the end, because these areas do not fall under any specific framework in the EC's system of external economic relations.)

These figures clearly show that the largest changes take place in relation to EFTA, Latin America, and the Middle East, in that order. However, despite the decline in EFTA's index, it remains first. Therefore, Spain and Portugal's incorporation into the Community may reduce the importance of developing relations with EFTA, a privileged partner. On the other hand, because the EC's trade dependence on the Middle East was much higher than on ACP or Mediterranean Policy countries even before the accession of Spain and Portugal, these figures may help the new entrants, in their efforts to show the other Ten the importance of developing formal relations with Middle East countries. Without detracting from the continuing importance that the Mediterranean Policy or the Lomé Convention has for Spain and Portugal (as witnessed by the slight increase of the indexes), Latin America could be singled out from the mass of GSP beneficiary countries for improved treatment.

Crude Oil and Gas Import Dependence on Different Geographic Areas or Producer Groups

Table 2.4 shows petroleum and petroleum product import dependence levels of Spain, Portugal, the EC-10, and the EC-12. (Care has been taken in each case to subtract imports from other present Community members.) Import ratios have been calculated in relation to different groupings selected for their political relevance: OPEC, the Middle East, Arab countries and Iran, and the Arab League.

From the table, there will be little substantial change in

Table 2.3
Index of Trade Vulnerability (1984)

	EC-10	EC-12	Change from EC-10 to EC-12
EFTA	41.91	40.32	−1.59
ACP	11.65	11.90	0.25
Mediterranean Policy countries	12.74	13.13	0.39
Latin America	12.32	13.38	1.06
Mid East	21.41	22.40	0.98

Source: Based on data from OECD Foreign Trade by Commodities.

Table 2.4
Import Dependence Levels of Petroleum
and Petroleum Products by Percentage (1984)[a]

	Spain[b]	Portugal[c]	EC-10[d]	EC-12
OPEC	64.95	83.75	77.38	76.08
Non-OECD Mid East	42.18	60.25	30.11	32.11
Arab countries and Iran	57.44	67.82	50.09	51.29
Arab countries	45.09	55.23	42.57	43.11

Source: OECD Foreign Trade by Commodities.
[a]Not including gas
[b]Excluding imports from Portugal and the EC
[c]Excluding imports from Spain and the EC
[d]Excluding imports from Spain, Portugal, and intra-EC trade

outside dependence levels with the Twelve as opposed to the Ten, especially regarding Arab countries. Interestingly, Spain's heavy reliance on Mexican crude oil results in a decline in the EC's dependence level on OPEC. As late as 1984, the Iranian factor would have led simultaneously to a higher dependence of the enlarged EC on Middle East crude oil, in comparison to what actually happened. This confirms the above comments concerning trade flows in general. Thus, contrary to what may be thought a priori, the increased vulnerability of the enlarged EC on the Mid East derives not from the two new members' reliance on Arab countries' oil supplies, but rather from their reliance on Iranian supplies.

Even then, however, the table does not explain the whole story, because the Ten relied much more on its own petroleum resources than did Spain and Portugal. For example, in 1984, the share of intra-EC imports of petroleum and petroleum products in total imports was 26.81%, whereas Spain and Portugal were importing 5.08% and 13.36% of their total oil imports from the EC-10. This difference in Spanish and Portuguese behavior, when compared to the Ten, only strengthens the above point on the Middle East. Recent statistics published by the Spanish National Institute of Hydrocarbons confirms our figures. In 1986, 32.9% of domestic crude oil consumption (by volume) originated in the Middle East, 32.53% from Africa, 22.52% from the Americas (of which 21.18% came from Mexico), and only 5.87% from the UK (none from Norway). That is, the enlarged EC is more dependent than the Ten on crude oil supplies from the Middle East, because extra-EC imports as a percentage of total imports increase from 73.2% to 75.4%.

Turning to natural and manufactured gas, Table 2.5 displays the import dependence levels of Spain, Portugal, the Ten, and the Twelve. (Here, too, care has been taken in each case to deduct imports originating in other EC member countries.) Because there are no imports from Iran, and because OPEC is not relevant in the case of gas, only figures from the Middle East and the Arab world as a whole have been given.

In the case of gas, the Twelve were clearly more dependent than the Ten on the two groupings selected, with dependence increasing most in relation to the Arab world, because of Spain's total reliance on Algerian and Libyan gas supplies. Portugal's record is a neutralizing factor, because it depends even less than the old EC on the two areas selected for study.

When intra-EC imports are considered as part of total gas imports, they account for 39.7% in the case of the Ten and only 12.38% in the case of Spain, but 87.07% in the Portuguese case. In this respect, because Spain and Portugal lie at opposite extremes, their inclusion in the EC implies only a slight increase in the reliance of the Twelve on external gas sources (from 60.29% to 60.93% of total imports), a small change in comparison with crude oil.

If present trends prevail in crude oil and gas imports, it would be logical for the enlarged EC to pay more attention to its relations with Iran, Libya, and Algeria. (Only Algeria has institutionalized relations with the EC under the Global Mediterranean Policy.)

Table 2.5
Import Dependence Levels of Gas
and Gas Products by Percentage (1984)

	Spain[a]	Portugal[b]	EC-10[c]	EC-12
Non-OECD				
Middle East	34.95	3.31	3.49	4.89
Arab countries	98.44	18.84	28.54	31.65

Source: OECD Foreign Trade by Commodities.
[a]Excluding imports from Portugal and the EC
[b]Excluding imports from Spain and EC
[c]Excluding imports from Spain, Portugal, and intra-EC trade

The Enlarged Community's
Quantum Leap in Tourism Activities

Until recently, the EC as an institution was not very active in tourism services. The Customs Union refers only to goods, whereas, in spite of the existence of several provisions in the Treaty of Rome relating to the right of establishment, trade in services was not an area of attention by the Community. The project of creating a true internal market by 1992 does, of course, have a bearing on the development of tourism as a service affected by nontariff barriers. Certainly, the deregulation of air transport in the EC and the elimination of tax-free shopping on intra-EC travel should have an impact on tourism-related activities.

The interest in tourism as an economic activity manifested by the Commission since 1986 has a great deal to do with Spain and Portugal's entry, because their inclusion makes a considerable difference to the Community as a whole. To be sure, this may have implications for future EC relations with nonmembers. For example, the creation of a true internal market for tourism and/or air transport can lead to both trade creation and trade diversion. Trade diversion may worry third countries, especially those in the Mediterranean (e.g., Turkey, Yugoslavia, Israel, and Morocco).[13] As has been stated,[14] if the Community does not do anything to prevent it, Spain and Portugal may actually lose visitors, probably to other Mediterranean countries. For, once Spain and Portugal adjust to the Common Agricultural Policy after the period of transition, food will become more expensive there than it is now, increasing the cost to prospective tourists. This would be the result of adopting CAP prices—which are well above the prevailing ones for goods on which the new EC members now have a comparative advantage (e.g., fruit, vegetables, and wine). On the other hand, the principle of Community preference leads to costly trade diversion effects (e.g., soya beans), which sometimes results in increases in consumer prices (on both goods for final or intermediary consumption). Here, the burden of trade diversion will be shared by the Spanish and Portuguese consumers with the tourists traveling in these two countries.

The expected increase in agricultural prices, together with an increase in road transport costs deriving from the adoption of strict EC regulations, may lead to a further boost in final consumer prices. Moreover, the project of harmonizing value added tax rates at the European level will in all probability lead to yet a further increase in the low tax rates currently applied on alcohol and tobacco by Spain and Portugal. According to press reports,[15] the Commission's pressure to harmonize VAT in the EC should increase current rates by 2.5% in Spain and 2.8% in Portugal. These two countries, together with Luxembourg and Greece, are expected to endure the largest rate increments. This would mean, for instance, that prices of table wine and beer in Spain would increase by 67% and 21%, respectively, and the price of spirits would rise by 88%.

Thanks to the free movement of goods and workers after the transition period, unitary labor costs between new members and old members will converge, which is what happened between Italy and its fellow EC members when the EC was created in 1958.[16] It may even be that the Spanish tourism boom of the 1960s had been bolstered by Italy's participation in the EC and that "reverse trade diversion" took place at that time.

If this reasoning is correct, Spain and Portugal—as enormous producers of tourism services—may try to counteract reverse trade diversion by suggesting that the EC implement regional liberalization of tourism services at the European level and/or of other activities related to tourism (e.g., currency regulations, charter regulations, etc). Consider the huge role played by Spain and Portugal in this area:[17]

- According to OECD figures, Spain's share of tourism payments in total exports of goods and services amounted to 19.9% in 1980 and Portugal's to 16.3%—as compared to 5.1% for France, 2.8% for Germany, and 8.5% for Italy.

- The Peninsula countries' share of expenditures in international tourism in total imports of goods and services was considerably under the EC average: 2.6% for Spain and 2.7% for Portugal—as compared with 8.9% for Germany and 3.6% for France.
- The share of international tourism receipts in the Gross Domestic Product (GDP) is above average in Spain and Portugal, compared to other EC members. Figures for 1985 are 6.1% for Spain, 7% for Portugal—as compared with 2.7% for the Ten.
- In the same year, the share of international tourism expenditures as a percentage of final private consumption was below the EC average: 1.3% for both Spain and Portugal—as compared with 3.5% for the Ten. Since domestic tourism does not seem to be affected by the EC, we only use figures for international tourism. However, international tourism is the dominant factor in total tourism for Portugal and for Spain, which is not the case for other European countries.
- According to Commission figures, full-time job equivalents generated by tourism expenditures were above the EC average: 9.1% for Spain, 8.6% for Portugal—as compared with 6% for the Ten. Of course, employment relates both to domestic and international tourism. Spain and Portugal had 18.1% of the total EC full-time job equivalents generated by tourism expenditures in 1985.
- When tourism (including domestic) receipts are considered, Spain and Portugal account for 12.1% of the figure for the Twelve, a figure which is raised to 21% when only international tourism receipts are considered. Here, it is interesting that the Peninsula countries account only for 3% of total expenditures for the Twelve.
- Spain and Portugal receive an above EC average of tourism receipts originating in other EC countries. In 1984 intra-Community tourism accounted for 61.7% of Spain's international tourism receipts and 53.4% of Portugal's—as compared with 46.4% for the Ten. Spain and Portugal accounted for 27% of intra-Community tourism receipts and only 15% of extra-EC tourism receipts in 1984. Another further indication of the importance of EC-originating tourism is that 78.4% of those visiting Spain in 1988 originated in the Community.

To sum up, Spain and Portugal are important producers of tourism services, representing 18% of total EC employment, 12% of total tourism receipts, and 21% of total EC international tourism receipts. International tourism receipts of the EC have increased by 27% since they joined, and employment has increased by 22%. Tourism attracted by Spain and Portugal is mainly Community oriented: the two countries generate 27% of total intra-EC receipts, an indicator of how much may be at stake for them. This may lead both governments to defend their positions in EC tourism markets, including, operation at the EC level.

Trade Dependence of the Outside World on the EC Before and After the Enlargement

An analysis of the fluctuation in trade dependence levels of third countries on the Community is critical if we are to assess possible changes in the demands that the Twelve will have to face from them. Table 2.6 sums up changes for those countries, which, for various (e.g., historical) reasons, the EC cannot ignore when it designs its foreign economic policies.

From this table, the countries for which levels of import dependence on the EC increase the most are Morocco, Tunisia, Egypt, and Libya, in that order. However, if we focus on the EC as a market—which is more important—Libya and Morocco increase their dependence the most, while Algeria registers a smaller increase in dependence, and Tunisia shows almost no increase. In terms of increased exports, Mexico is third and Egypt fourth. By region, the Maghreb seems to be the most affected by the entry of Spain and Portugal, although it is followed closely by the Mashrek. The level of export dependence of ACP countries in relation to Spain and Portugal is higher than the same figure for Latin America. However, the EC market becomes more important for Latin America, and much less so for EFTA countries or the U.S.

Changes in the Political Structure of the European Parliament

Using data from 1985 and 1986, as given in Table 2.7, one can analyze how the ideological map of the Community was affected right after the last Enlargement. Note that the Spanish and

Table 2.6
Import (M) and Export (X) Levels of Dependence
of Selected Third Countries by Percentage (1984)

	EC-10		EC-12		Spain		Portugal	
	M	X	M	X	M	X	M	X
Morocco	34.49	50.58	43.83	59.42	8.42	7.87	0.92	0.97
Algeria	58.39	53.40	62.28	57.91	3.53	3.77	0.36	0.74
Tunisia	57.80	57.52	64.14	58.35	6.02	0.73	0.32	0.10
Maghreb	52.75	53.52	58.35	58.19	5.11	3.97	0.49	0.70
Egypt	34.59	58.41	39.47	64.18	4.69	5.41	0.19	0.36
Syria	21.26	38.13	23.29	40.88	1.88	2.38	0.15	0.37
Lebanon	42.99	7.15	46.75	7.22	3.69	0.07	0.07	[a]
Jordan	26.81	5.42	28.08	5.47	1.11	0.05	0.16	[a]
Mashrek	33.14	44.66	37.04	48.73	3.73	3.77	0.17	0.30
Israel	37.36	32.48	38.41	34.06	0.90	0.51	0.15	1.07
Turkey	28.23	37.86	31.47	38.68	3.07	0.41	0.17	0.41
Yugoslavia	29.68	25.72	30.28	25.83	0.51	0.09	0.09	0.02
Cyprus	53.99	28.03	56.75	28.30	2.26	0.27	0.50	[a]
Malta	77.09	68.15	79.20	68.25	1.84	0.06	0.27	0.04
MPC	41.52	46.91	45.43	50.69	3.63	3.14	0.28	0.64
Lybia	55.56	61.10	59.84	70.49	4.26	9.21	0.02	0.18
Arab world	34.64	29.23	37.27	34.07	2.46	4.06	0.17	0.78
United States	17.66	21.55	18.58	23.16	0.77	1.17	0.15	0.44
Mexico	10.99	10.57	12.42	18.25	1.43	7.26	[a]	0.42
Argentina	24.46	25.49	26.53	29.53	2.03	2.97	0.04	1.07
Latin America	16.43	18.98	18.02	22.65	1.54	3.14	0.05	0.53
Switzerland	67.26	50.38	69.01	52.95	1.42	1.96	0.33	0.61
Austria	60.50	53.39	61.51	55.14	0.65	1.51	0.36	0.24
Sweden	52.74	47.91	54.56	49.35	1.05	1.14	0.77	0.30
Finland	35.41	37.88	36.97	38.82	0.91	0.73	0.65	0.21
Norway	45.59	69.88	47.15	70.62	0.84	0.34	0.72	0.40
EFTA	55.30	51.99	56.90	53.61	1.04	1.22	0.56	0.40
ACP[b]	35.57	45.25	38.20	50.23	1.88	3.86	0.75	1.12

Source: IMF-Direction of Trade Statistics Yearbook, 1985. OECD Foreign Trade by Commodities, 1986 (Export, Import).
[a]Data not available
[b]The ACP was calculated only with 52 countries. Botswana, Comoros, Kiribati, Lesotho, Swaziland, Tonga, Tovalu, and Upper Volta were not calculated because of lack of data

Table 2.7
Political Affiliation of Representatives to the European
Parliament Before and After the Enlargement by Percentage

	1985	1986	Difference
Socialists	29.95	33.20	+3.25
European People's Party	25.11	22.77	−2.34
European Democrats	11.52	12.16	+0.64
Communists	9.90	8.88	−1.02
Liberal Democrats and Reform	7.14	8.10	−0.96
European Alliance for Renewal	6.91	6.56	−0.35
Rainbow	4.37	3.86	−0.51
European Right	3.68	3.08	−0.60
Nonaffiliated	1.38	1.35	−0.03

Portuguese data to calculate the new shares of each political group at the European Parliament are those prevailing in early 1986. It is to be recalled that, for a transitory period, Spanish and Portuguese political parties were represented at the European Parliament in the same proportions as those prevailing at the time in their own national parliaments. From Table 2.7 it is obvious that the Socialist group increased its representation to the detriment of almost all other groups, including all parties that lean toward the right. This is not surprising given that 42 out of the 84 new members of the European Parliament (i.e., 50%) joined the Socialist group. As a result the comfortable center-right majority (composed of the Christian Democrats, Conservatives, and Liberals), which had prevailed for a long time, was seriously eroded, almost leading to a loss of its majority status.[18]

Only in 1987 did the two new member countries organize direct elections of their representatives to the European Parliament. (European-wide elections were scheduled to take place only in June 1989.) The 1987 elections served to confirm the shift of the European Parliament to the left as a consequence of the Enlargement. This is shown in Column (1) of Table 2.8. The slight decrease of the Socialist group was compensated by a comeback of the Communists.

If the focus is placed instead on the June 1989 direct elections to the European Parliament (Table 2.8, column (2)), the shift to the left is again confirmed, although caution is requested when using these last figures. They may reflect a general swing of the European electorates to the left quite unconnected with the Enlargement. Comparisons between the two columns are also difficult to make, since a series of regroupings have taken place in view of the 1989 elections.

As far as the EC's institutionalized relations with third countries are concerned, the change in the ideological map could imply an increased awareness in the European Parliament of the problems and needs confronting developing countries (including ACP, Mediterranean, and Latin American countries), for example, in the domain of foreign debt or of improvement in the EC's Generalized System of Preferences. This clashes with what is suggested later in the analyses of the changes in the balance between the development of external and domestic policies of the EC. In any case, these political shifts have already had an inpact on EC domestic affairs, particularly in the reform of the Common Agricultural Policy engaged in

Table 2.8
Political Affiliation of Representatives to the
European Parliament After the First Two Direct
Elections in Spain and Portugal by Percentage

	(1)	(2)
Socialists	32.05	34.75
European People's Party	21.62	23.36
European Democrats	12.74	6.56
Communists	9.27	8.11
Liberals Democrats and Reform	8.69	9.65
European Alliance for Renewal	5.79	3.86
Rainbow	3.86	2.12
Greens	—	5.79
European Right	3.09	3.28
Non-affiliated	2.90	2.12

early 1988. The traditional reliance on guaranteed prices is being replaced by measures directed to structural reform in depressed agricultural regions under the unremitting pressure of Spanish, Greek, and Portuguese socialists.

The Overseas Image of the Enlarged Community as Perceived in Brussels

Although the manner in which the image of the EC Twelve, as compared to that of the Ten, will differ in the eyes of nonmember countries cannot be understood until well into the 1990s, several EC, Spanish and Portuguese officials were asked what they thought the differences would be. It should be stressed here that these officials were not asked what third countries or EC officials expected from Spain and Portugal, but rather how they felt the inclusion of these two countries would change the total picture of the entire Community. Although the results presented are piecemeal and incomplete, they help draw a tentative, and unconsolidated, image of the Twelve. (The persons interviewed are among those given in the bibliography.)

Apparently, there is a shared perception in nonmember countries that the enlarged EC represents a more impressive trading bloc than the Ten, and that it must be respected more than previously. Clearly, the Community's reputation as a successful economic model of integration has improved, because more countries are finding it beneficial to join. Moreover, third countries that cannot or do not want to enter the EC may be tempted to emulate the model, which may place the Community in the role of advisor to or sponsor of similar regional schemes.

Beyond this, a distinction must be made between developed and developing countries. For example, the Third World, particularly Central America and the Arab world, expects more from the Twelve than from the Ten. On their hand, ACP countries follow EC fisheries policies very closely—because Spain fishes along the African coast. They would like to encourage the establishment of processing plants in Africa, rather than in Spain or Portugal.

In the Mediterranean, the change in the size and structure of the EC is perceived as increasing its role in the area, an idea that began developing at the beginning of the 1980s. This does not, however, mean that the change is seen as positive, because some Mediterranean countries view the Enlargement as a menace, particularly in the long term. While these same countries understand the political aim of stabilizing democracies in Southern Europe by integrating them into the EC, they have some questions regarding the role that Spain and Portugal will play in Brussels, particularly after 1990, or certainly after 1996, by which time all the provisions of the Treaty of Accession will be working in favor of Spanish and Portuguese agriculture. In ACP countries, the fear is that the Third World may be neglected, for the EC now has its own South; they fear huge domestic programs may absorb a higher share of the budget. Finally, the EC appears to be displaying an ever-growing political consensus on many subjects.

For developed countries, in particular for EFTA countries like Norway and Sweden, the enlarged EC is viewed as more attractive than the Ten, which may help strengthen the position of those in their governments who are considering joining the EC. The same is true of Morocco. Here the incentive is not the increased size of the EC market, but the concrete presence of the Iberian Peninsula in the Community. (More will be said on this subject in Chapter 4.) U.S. views will also be treated separately in that chapter, because of the particular role of the United States as a superpower involved indirectly in the negotiations that led to the accession of Spain and Portugal. The perspective from the outside contrasts sharply with that of officials who work in the Commission, and who perceive the enlarged Community as being weakened, at least in the short run, by new debates on budgetary- and agricultural-related problems between the EC's

North and South. In general, they view the larger number of members as creating more difficulties in arriving at common positions. All this implies that the economic benefits expected by the Third World may not come about. And, although the Community is certainly more sensitive than before to the political problems of Mediterranean and Middle Eastern countries, given the EC's own fragility and vulnerability, it cannot do very much to help promote peace or to increase economic stability in these areas. The same holds true with regard to Central America.

3

The Global Impact of New Member Countries on the Community's External Economic Policymaking

The Key Variables

Before looking at the intentions of the two new EC members insofar as the development of the Community's system of foreign economic relations is concerned, some preliminary questions must be addressed: Will the new entrants have any real influence at all? Will their presence in EC institutions really make a difference? Do they have the means to defend their policies? What is their weight in the Community? What happened when other countries entered the Community? These questions are examined in the following pages, along with the issue of the principles and grand designs that determine the foreign policies—including trade and development assistance policies—of all countries, and of Spain and Portugal in particular.

A related subject—an assessment of the importance that the two countries in question and the Community as a whole attach to foreign policy—will also be taken up. Thus, by the end of Chapter 3, the reader should be able to assess the difference that the Enlargement from the Ten to the Twelve might make as viewed from a global perspective. The question of regional considerations will be the task of Chapter 4.

Before concluding Chapter 3, we will present an assessment of the likelihood that a southern lobby be created in the EC and what the current views of Spain are on this subject.

Relative Population and GNP

One way to assess the weight of any given country in the international arena is to consider its share of the total GNP of the group under consideration, that is, its economic weight. Another way is to assess that country's demographic and political weight, by using relative population figures. In Table 3.1, the corresponding shares for Spain, Portugal, and the two countries together are considered, as are the shares of different combinations of Mediterranean member countries. The latter is of particular importance in view of the possibility of future alliances among these countries.

Focusing on GNP share, it would appear that Portugal's weight is negligible, and that even Spain's share is low in comparison with the theoretical share, 8.3%, which each of Twelve might have if all countries' GNP were equal. Thus, if the new entrants are to impress other member countries, they will have to find allies. But, in this respect, adding Greece does not really change things, for in economic terms the creation of a Mediterranean lobby, which has at times been suggested, does not seem to carry enough weight without the participation of both Italy and France.

The panorama has a slightly different look when the focus is directed to population. For here, Spain is among the big European countries, while Portugal clearly falls into the category of the smaller members. This is probably why the former has been assigned an intermediary position in various EC institutions. Note, too, that together the two new entrants represent almost

Table 3.1
Share of the EC's GNP and Population (by percentage, 1986)

	Share of GNP	Share of Population
Spain	6.5	12.0
Portugal	0.8	3.2
Spain and Portugal	7.3	15.2
Spain, Portugal, and Greece	8.7	18.2
Spain, Portugal, Greece, and Italy	25.5	36.0
Five Mediterranean EC members	45.9	53.2

one-sixth of the total EC population. And, given the higher than EC average birthrates in these two countries, that share should increase in the next decade. Even now, however, if we group them with Greece and Italy, this share more than doubles without considering France. Thus, since 1986, the Mediterranean members of the EC have become an entity that will have to be reckoned with—if they form a united front.

Weight of Spain and Portugal in EC Institutions

As shown in Table 3.2, the importance of the Iberian countries varies slightly according to the institution considered. Consider, especially with respect to possible future alliances: the five Mediterranean members of the EC currently account for more than half of the total voting power in the European Parliament, where decisions are taken by simple majority.[19] Together, Spain and Portugal can elect a higher number of Euro-deputies (84) than the UK (81), another indication of their clout.

Before proceeding, however, it must be stressed that the figures presented in the table should be used with caution, particularly in reference to the European Parliament. This is due to the unlikelihood of all the members of a single country's delegation voting the same way on an issue.[20] (Different ideologies are represented in their delegations.) Obviously, this is even less likely when one considers large categories like "Mediterranean countries." Moreover, national voting disappears completely in the Court of Justice, which is totally independent of national governments.

The figures in Table 3.2 have more value with regard to the Commission, and particularly to the Council of Ministers— Spain carries the same weight as larger countries in both of these, despite its relatively small share of the total EC GNP. For instance, Spain elects two members to the Commission, the same as any other large country in the EC. Although this might imply a slight upward bias favoring Spain's influence in EC decisionmaking, it should also be noted that Commissioners are supposed to work toward the good of the entire Community, ignoring their country of origin in their decisionmaking. Nonetheless, since recent experience shows that Commissioners

Table 3.2
Share in EC Decisionmaking Power by Percentage

	Council of Ministers	Commission	Parliament	Court of Justice
Spain	10.52	11.76	11.58	7.69
Portugal	6.57	5.88	4.63	7.69
Spain and Portugal	17.10	17.64	16.21	15.38
EC Medit. Members	50.00	47.05	52.12	38.46

do not always ignore the interests of their own countries—in which they have been political personalities and in which they still have political ambitions after they leave the Commission—this bias favoring Spain may carry some weight.

There are occasions when even the smallest member in terms of GNP (e.g., Luxembourg) can exert disproportionate influence, for example, during the six months when each EC member occupies the presidency of the Council of Ministers, which stretches for some matters to 18 months (when the half year preceding and following the actual presidency are taken into consideration). A good example of this is the Euro-Arab dialogue, in which the highest level of representation on the European side is held by a troika composed of the Council's current president, previous president and the next in line. Thus even tiny Portugal can advance or block programs and projects during the period of its presidency.

Spain has held the presidency of the Council since January 1989. Two camps emerged in the planning stages of Spanish strategy for their presidency. One group wanted Spain to assume an activist role, making its mark on the EC's basic orientations[21]; the other, which was more experienced with the inner workings of the Community and which eventually dominated the debate, felt that it would be better for Spain's image to be more conservative with the agenda and to show effective consistency during its presidency. Those in favor of a low-key presidency eventually won out, stressing that a successful presidency is one that makes progress with negotiations and business initiated by previous presidencies. As an example of the dominance of the latter view, the Spanish presidency successfully concluded an economic agreement between Poland and the EC, even though Eastern European relations are not a priority for Spain. A realistic view was even adopted by Spain regarding EC relations with Central America, an area where Spain's desire to leave an imprint is paramount.

Finally, from an institutional viewpoint, the reforms approved in the Single European Act do not act to completely suppress what is called the Luxembourg compromise, for every EC member can still exercise the traditional veto power possibility when things come to the test (although not on many matters related to the EC's internal market).

From the above, clearly, the voices of the two new entrants cannot be ignored, and at least theoretically, they—along with all other EC members—can influence EC decisions. Certainly, there must be the political will to exert this power, which depends on the importance a particular subject has for the member country involved.

Knowing how to cooperate with other member countries also determines the impact of a country on the EC and its institutions.[22] In general, Spaniards working for the Commission have the impression that the UK, France, and the Federal Republic of Germany—the three biggest members—have a direct influence in shaping its policies and decisions. When the three agree on an issue, all other members must align themselves with them; when they disagree, mainly on secondary matters, Spain may be able to exert an influence. For instance, these officials point out that Latin American and fisheries policies would not be on the agenda as often without Spain's relentless pressure. Of course, as in any other international institution, the influence that a country has depends heavily on the quality of its representatives. In this respect, various officials agree that the professional abilities of the Spaniards at the Commission is very high, and that they bring with them a lot of Europeanism, youth and imagination. However, as in the past, this may change over time, as they realize the degree of politicization that pervades the Commission's work. But, some observers say, this increased cynicism will be offset when Spanish and Portuguese manpower is fully deployed in 1993. For in contrast the very high profile of Dutch and Belgian officials, Spaniards and Portuguese do not yet occupy important positions in the Community's overseas delegations. Spaniards assert this is bound to change. Spanish influence in the EC's external affairs is bound to increase substantially as a result of the reshuffle of portfolios in the new EC Commission named for a period of four years starting on January 1, 1989. The two Spaniards who were responsible for domestic affairs in the previous Commission have been reassigned to management of EC relations with Mediterranean, Latin American, and Asian countries and cooperation and development (which basically involves supervising relations with ACP countries). A caveat, however, is that according to the EC treaties commissioners are supposed to work for the welfare of the Community as a unit without unduly favoring their country of origin.

The British and Greek Precedents

In order to estimate how the entry of Spain and Portugal into the EC might change the Community's shaping of external economic relations, we can look at what happened when other countries joined.

There is no doubt that British influence has been substantial in the design of various Community policies. For example, the uncompromising attitude of the UK played a large part in eliminating reverse tariff preferences in EC Cooperation agreements signed with Maghreb and Mashrek countries in the mid-1970s. In this respect, Britain has always been quite receptive to the demands for non-reciprocity advanced by developing countries in international forums. The conclusion of Free Trade Agreements between the EC and individual EFTA countries was one of the few conditions that the UK succeeded in imposing on the Six, and this was a quid pro quo for British acceptance of the acquis communautaire upon her accession. Also, as is well known, the CAP reform was initiated under British pressure and its implementation takes place under constant British scrutiny.

It has also been said that European Political Cooperation (EPC) was an outcome of the First Enlargement. In any case, it is inconceivable that EPC would have been achieved without the active participation of a European power as large as Britain. Moreover, fears that lukewarm British attitudes toward the EC in the 1970s would harm the development of EPC also proved unfounded. Certainly, even together, Spain and Portugal do not appear to possess the political clout that would allow them to have as much leverage as the UK on EC decisionmaking; however, as shown below, they do not lag far behind.

At the opposite extreme, tiny (in terms of GNP and population) Greece was able to alter EC decisions relating mainly, but not entirely, to the Middle East and Turkey. For example, in December 1983, Greece succeeded in stopping its nine EC partners from issuing a joint declaration openly condemning the USSR in the Korean airliner affair. In general, whenever Greece did not have the backing of at least one or two other member countries, some of the radical views expressed by the former socialist Greek government in EC caucuses were viewed by other members as a mere nuisance, and were ignored.

Spanish and Portuguese Views on Trade and Aid Policies

Trade

In spite of the important inroads made by liberal-minded people in the shaping of Spain's trade diplomacy, traditionally it has been characterized by a mercantilistic-protectionistic element. Portugal, on the other hand, has had a much more varied record in this area. For over a century, its politicians have been highly aware of the advantages of free trade for a small and poor country. However, concerning manufactured products and services, the Iberian members will align themselves with those who are trying to keep EC borders as closed as possible to outside exporters. This is not only because, as mentioned earlier, traditionally they have been protectionistic, but also because both countries believe that opening their domestic markets to other EC members—an inescapable consequence of their entry into the Community—should make them extra cautious vis-a-vis new initiatives such as including services in the GATT, eliminating the Multi-Fibre Arrangement (MFA), and further liberalizing the EC's GSP scheme. Of course, the completion of the Internal Market by 1992 will only strengthen this line of argument. For, given that the intention is to have a real Common Commercial Policy by then, Spain and Portugal cannot ask for special treatment insofar as their relations with third countries are concerned. Thus, the EC will have to take their interests very seriously when it shapes its position regarding nonmembers.

In this connection, one of Spain's arguments will be that, as forecast, its trade balance with the EC sharply deteriorated beginning in early 1986, because imports increased by 31.6% whereas exports rose by only 6.8%. Globally, there was a 12.5% increase in the trade deficit, with 1986 exports covering only

77.7% of imports, as compared with 80.9% in 1985. This trend continued throughout 1987, when the deficit reached $12.84 billion, doubling from the previous year, with imports from the Community increasing by 33.9% in that year alone whereas exports increased by only 16.8%. Between 1985 and 1987 the trade deficit with the Community increased fourfold.[23] The same pattern repeated itself in 1988 when the trade deficit reached the record level of $17.55 billion, an increase of 36.7% over 1987, and if it continues in the coming years, one should not expect Spain to be overly enthusiastic about further liberalization of imports from non-EC countries. Spain, for example, is apprehensive regarding plans to eliminate barriers on intra-EC trade in services. If this is so regarding *domestic* EC trade, more caution from Spain in areas such as GATT discussions on trade in services can be expected.

Basically, the same is true of Portugal. A Foreign Ministry report on Portugal's first year in the European Community warned that GATT negotiations on agricultural products should not be allowed to decrease the protection of Portugal's agriculture resulting from the Accession Treaty.[24] With regard to trade in services, the report points out that the EC must adopt a long-term perspective, probably implying that it should delay full liberalization for the foreseeable future.

As far as agriculture is concerned, there are two arguments that lead to contradictory conclusions. One is that, like Italy, Spain might press for more protection in CAP, on the basis that, over the years, Mediterranean produce has been disadvantaged by this policy.[25] Spain will propose the inclusion of new products in the CAP, or the expansion of the periods covered by the reference price system, or more subsidies for processing activities in the producing country, Spain. On the other hand, as heavy importers of grain and meat, both Portugal and Spain are aware that present CAP policies lead to costly trade diversion losses. In this sense, they share Britain's interest in liberalizing CAP. The fact is that official circles, at least in Spain, have not followed this line to date, probably because the impact of CAP itself on consumer prices has not yet been felt, and will not be felt for several years, partially because it is spread over a number of years. Surely, as time passes, voices in Spain—including those in the European Parliament—will increasingly question the over-protection of continental products built into CAP (as is the case with Britain today).

At least, in the short run, Spain seems more inclined toward increasing the protection of Mediterranean agriculture within the EC than toward reducing the protection offered to continental (e.g., grain and meat) products. This may be accomplished in a roundabout way (e.g., as is explained below in my remarks on cohesion)—by securing an increase in structural expenditures from the EC for regions cultivating fruit and vegetables. In this context, it is perhaps worth recalling that, once Greece realized that Spanish membership in the EC and the concomitant revision of the Mediterranean Policy were inevitable, as well as that a more protectionist CAP was not likely, it used all its leverage to get the so-called Integrated Mediterranean Programs approved. The Greeks' purpose was to restructure their outdated agriculture with the help of massive funding from the EC. Of course, Greece was backed by Italy and France. And, with two more Mediterranean countries in the Community, there is always the possibility that this pattern could be repeated by pressing the Northern members of the Community to approve new aid to Southern members, as a reward for the latter's acceptance of new candidates for membership.

Another dimension of EC trade policies that is likely to be influenced by the new members is the Community's multiple trade discrimination policy toward nonmembers. As George Yannopoulos emphasizes,[26] both countries, but particularly Spain, are likely to strengthen this policy rather than push the EC toward multilateralism, for this will allow them to exert influence by distributing favors and privileges, especially to their former colonies.

Aid

As far as pressing for more aid to non-EC members, neither Spain nor Portugal are in any position to push for this in Brussels, because neither devotes a significant share of its GNP to this aim. For example, in 1987, a year after entering into the EC, Spain still devoted a mere 0.12% of its GNP to Official Development Assistance (ODA). Table 3.3 gives for comparative purposes the amounts of ODA distributed in 1984 by Development Assistance Committee (DAC) members of the EC, Spain, and Portugal, as well as the percentage of the GNP that these amounts represent. A glance at the table shows that even Spain's $157 million was only 0.10% of its GNP, which was far from the DAC members' average of 0.36%. It is also noteworthy that Ireland and Italy, whose per capita GNPs are comparable to that of Spain,

Table 3.3
Official Development Assistance in 1984
(in millions of dollars and as
a percentage of GNP)

	ODA	% of GNP
Holland	1209	0.97
Denmark	438	0.83
France	3833	0.78
Belgium	435	0.56
West Germany	2880	0.46
Britain	1462	0.34
Italy	1116	0.32
Ireland	36	0.23
Spain	157	0.10
Portugal	8	a

Source: Anuario El País, 1986.
[a]Insignificant

allot two and three times as much of their GNP to development
assistance.

In the period 1981–87, Spain's average ODA as a percentage
of GNP has fluctuated considerably, and—its frequent
declarations notwithstanding—there are no signs of an upward
trend. In Table 3.4 we show Spain's ODA to nonmembers of the
EC, and its total flows of dollars—including direct investments
and export credits—to developing countries, as percentages of its
GNP.

From these figures, we can see that the share of ODA in
Spain's GNP has gone down and then up; but that, when total
resources are considered, there is a sharp downward trend. In the
past the Spanish Development Aid Fund (FAD), has played a
leading role in Spain's ODA. Created in 1976, this fund's role is
bound to decrease now that Spain has joined the EC, because it
must now grant the European Development Fund (EDF) an
equivalent of 70% of the FAD. According to the Treaty of
Accession, Spain must deposit a total of ECU 499.8 million in the
sixth EDF (1985–1990), all of which is devoted to aid to ACP
countries. This implies an annual amount of more than $100
million, as compared with the 1984 ODA of $157 million shown in
Table 3.3. When we look at the programs presented in 1985,
Spain's ODA share of the GNP should have reached 0.15% by 1987
but, as shown in Table 3.4, this goal was not achieved. The
present Socialist government has pledged to boost this relatively
low percentage by 1992, so as to reach the DAC's average, and to

Table 3.4
Spain's ODA and Total Funds to Developing Countries as a Percentage of GNP

	1981	1982	1983	1984	1985	1986	1987
ODA	0.13	0.13	0.04	0.09	0.10	0.09	0.12
Total Resources	1.13	1.30	0.66	0.10	0.22	n.a.	n.a.

Source: *Boletín ICE*, various numbers.
n.a. = not available

join the DAC in the not-too-distant future. Confirmation of these intentions can be found in the resolutions adopted at the Socialist party's 1984 Congress,[27] calling for 0.3% of the GNP as the short-term aid aim, with a final objective of 0.7%. But no date has been established for this impressive figure, and the guidelines of the 1984 Congress stipulates that Spain's ODA must take its economic possibilities and capabilities into account. This means, in particular, that the destination and contents of development cooperation will be aimed at countries that can make use of Spain's intermediate technologies.

Spain's Socialist government has also been directed to ensure that its ODA fosters freedom, democracy, and social justice, as well as economic growth. As Secretary of State for International Cooperation and for Iberoamerica, Luis Yañez, has noted, Spain's views on Third World affairs will be guided by ethical, as well as economic, components. And Enrique Barón, another important member of the Socialist party, who became President of the European Parliament in July 1989, has called development aid one of the policies of the European Community that must be defended and reinforced.[28]

Spanish leaders are well aware that there will be restrictions on that portion of their aid to developing countries that is channelled through the EC. Thus, Spain's contributions to the EDF will benefit only one of the countries on its official list of priorities, its former colony Equatorial Guinea. But it will also strive to somehow associate the Dominican Republic within future EC-ACP Conventions, on the basis that this Caribbean nation shares the island of Hispaniola with Haiti, which does hold observer status at the Lomé III Convention.

Other candidates to receive Spain's bilateral ODA are countries in Central America; Bolivia, Peru, and Ecuador; the Maghreb (including Mauritania); the Portuguese-speaking countries in Africa; and the Philippines.

In contrast to being on the receiving end in the 1970s, Portugal is now called upon to act more like other developed countries. Interestingly, however, Portugal was a member of the OECD's DAC prior to 1974, because of its massive aid—in terms of GNP—to its colonies in Africa. As indicated in Table 3.3, Portuguese ODA is very limited, and what little aid is given is mainly directed to former colonies, particularly Angola, Mozambique and, especially in recent years, to the Cape Verde Islands.[29] Less than 10% of Portugal's ODA was devoted to other developing countries in 1986, as indicated in Table 3.5.

To sum up, if all of Spain's plans to increase bilateral and multilateral ODA do come to fruition, by the mid-1990s, Spain should be able to make its voice heard on EC aid policy. Conversely, Portugal will not be able to influence the Community's aid policies in the foreseeable future.

Relative Weight of Foreign and Domestic Affairs in the Enlarged Community

The level of ODA of the Twelve in comparison with the Ten will depend on how much importance the two new entrants place on foreign affairs in general, and whether the enlarged EC will have sufficient resources at its disposal to continue developing its external relations in coming years.

The first point must be treated with caution, as Spain did not give priority to diplomacy or foreign affairs under the long dictatorship of General Francisco Franco. As some experts have stressed, although Spain exhibited a natural vocation as a sea power several centuries ago, it has behaved with a continental mentality for more than 150 years.[30] And, during the Franco period, foreign policy was the *domaine reservé* of the Caudillo, who used it mainly to preserve his power. This long-term lack of interest in foreign affairs extended throughout almost the entire period of Spain's transition to democracy, until it entered NATO and became a member of the European Community. Thus, between 1975 and 1981, foreign affairs did not hold a central place in Spanish politics, as domestic political and economic matters were dominating the local scene.

Until the government of Leopoldo Calvo-Sotelo applied for Spain's entry into NATO in the early 1980s, there was an unofficial consensus among Spanish political parties to continue the inherited *status quo* in foreign policy matters. Party leaders

Table 3.5
Distribution of Portuguese Economic
Aid (1986, in millions of escudos)

Cape Verde Islands	266.6
Angola	34.4
Mozambique	29.8
Guinea Bissau	24.6
St. Tome/Principe	23.4
Multilateral Cooperation	10.1
Other developing countries	30.2
TOTAL	419.0

felt that domestic affairs had to be stressed, so that, when Spain did draw up a new foreign policy, it would be one that befitted a democratic country of Southern Europe. Spain's lack of experience in international affairs was another factor that—although recognized by all political forces—led to some controversial and essentially inconsequential steps in foreign policy during the Suárez government (e.g., Spain's observer status at the nonaligned countries' conference in Havana in 1979). But, once the transition to democracy was successfully achieved, there has been a remarkable change in Spain's attitude toward foreign affairs, particularly since the end of 1982, when the Socialist party was voted into power.

A survey of party programs and interviews reveal that Spain now has the political will to strive for "the place it merits" in the international arena, namely, a middle power in Southern Europe that can exercise influence in Africa, Latin America, and the Middle East. Also new horizons must be opened in Pacific Basin countries such as Japan, China, and Indonesia, as well as in sub-Saharan Africa,[31] and Spanish culture must be spread. As stressed by former Socialist Foreign Minister Fernando Morán, Spain's international inferiority complex should be replaced, for it is unjustified in light of the more than 300 million people around the world who speak its language. This opinion is shared by right-wingers such as Daniel Valcarcel, the editor of the prestigious journal on world affairs, *Política Exterior*, who has stated, "Spain has an international influence that is not [being] exerted today."[32]

The resources for this political expansion exist, but they must be mobilized if this task is to be accomplished. However, a learning period must be granted. One of the first priorities (if Spain wants to become an actor with a role on the international scene) is to somehow change the inward-looking reflexes that still exist among certain Spaniards. For example, during the debates over the Atlantic Alliance, those opposed to Spain's entering NATO constantly reiterated the argument that "leaning backwards" may have been the reason why Spain was able to remain neutral—and, incidentally, to do big business— during the two wars that tore Europe asunder. As *The Economist* of July 18, 1987, put it, Spain "is still distinguished from its main European partners by its parochial attitude towards Western security." Thus integration into the EC is precisely what is needed to open the eyes of the Spanish people to the outside world— and not only toward the South, but to the East as well. In 1986, Francisco Granell, now a Director General at the EC Commission, suggested that integration into the EC implies Spain's comeback as "a fragment of a superpower," instead of a country playing at best a secondary role on the international scene.[33] All this neglects the basic fact that Spain's membership in the EC requires an increasing share of its human and financial resources be put at the disposal of the Ministry of Foreign Affairs and other ministries, like Agriculture. Indeed, the Spanish embassy in Brussels is now by far the largest Spanish representation abroad, with a greater investment there than in its Washington embassy. Moreover, one of the Ministry of Foreign Affairs' three secretariats of state deals exclusively with EC activities.

Portugal is another story. Experts interviewed agree that its ancestral fear of Spain has pushed the country toward the Atlantic Ocean, obliging it to develop intensive relations with the United Kingdom, and more recently, with France and the United States. Thus, Portugal was a founding member of both NATO and EFTA. Moreover, its colonial past in Africa has given it a taste for Third World matters. But, despite this predisposition toward foreign affairs, Portugal has been involved in so many internal crises since the 1974 Revolution that there has been little time left to develop external relations. Added to this are domestic economic problems so pressing that Portugal is still in many respects a developing country.

Taking the above into consideration, one is tempted to predict that—at least in the short term—the EC Twelve will be more cautious than the Ten in its foreign relations. The new entrants' limited exposure to international affairs renders them less than an asset to the Community in this respect. Also consider, the EC will be absorbed, both by budgetary- and agricultural-related problems deriving in part from the Enlargement and in part by programs working toward the completion of the Internal Market. For, not only will Spain and Portugal request the Community's help in adjusting their economies to increased competition from the North, but industrial and farm sectors that feel menaced by expanded imports from the Iberian Peninsula are likely to ask Brussels' support after the transition period.

One possibility—for which there are many precedents—is to increase the barriers faced by nonmembers. As Yannopoulos points out,[34] the failure of other EC countries to adjust to competition from the Italian footwear sector led the EC to increase protection on footwear imports from nonmembers. This is what happened also with steel products, where strong internal EC competition led to increased protectionism. And, even while the negotiations for the latest Enlargement were still in progress, the EC Commission formulated plans to restrict soya oil imports, mainly from the United States, to make room for Spanish olive oil in EC markets. For these reasons and others, the Twelve will be less willing to develop new external policies and will have fewer resources to devote to this purpose.[35] Thus, before considering new candidates such as Turkey or Austria for membership, the EC must first adjust to the new conditions brought about by the accession of Spain and Portugal.

Many have predicted that the last Enlargement will lead to a new North-South division within the European Community, which could have a disrupting effect in the early 1990s.[36] Since new voting rules came into effect in July 1987, with the Single European Act—whereby, in most cases, individual members cannot veto Community projects—they have to form blocs in order to do so. In economic matters, the inclination may be for poor members to band together, and, with the exception of Ireland, all the poor members are Southern European countries. In Spain some individuals speak about a periphery of northern Mediterranean members to be added to the external periphery of southern Mediterranean nonmembers. Sharp divergences of opinion among EC policymakers exist on this point. Some specialists insist that Portugal will not vote with Mediterranean countries on political or many economic matters. Moreover, while Spain, Italy, and Greece seem to be working together on economic issues, France often votes differently. This seems to lend credence to the opinions of experts who dismiss talk of the creation of a Southern bloc: similar forecasts when Greece joined the EC proved unfounded. But other experts interviewed tend to think otherwise, pointing to the cooperation between Greece, France, and Italy that led these countries to extract the Integrated Mediterranean Programs from Northern EC members.

The truth probably lies somewhere in between. For, as some officials have said, Spain is not in favor of a Southern lobby because, instead of helping develop active policies, it would lead to defensive actions.[37] A clear example of the latter tendency has been going on since shortly after Spain joined the EC, when it adopted the view, shared by the Commission itself, that creating an internal market would only broaden the economic gap between poor and rich members, and that this tendency should be offset by voluntary measures promoting more cohesion within the Community. This sentiment was echoed by Spanish Prime Minister Felipe Gonzalez, when he said that he favors the creation of a social, economic, and cultural space in Europe, and not merely the creation of an internal market.[38] If such cohesion is to be attained, there must be much more solidarity than now exists among EC members, and in Gonzalez's view, the internal market project risks creating a dual economy within the EC itself. Spain, he continued, is already making a tremendous contribution toward such cohesion by opening its economy to other EC members and by eliminating tariffs, thereby increasing their rate of growth. The elimination of additional trade barriers on the imports of other EC members without sufficient help to facilitate adjustment would put the Spanish economy in an untenable position. And, as other highly placed Spanish officials point out, their country is against a European Community "a la carte."

The reform of the Common Agricultural Policy, approved in February 1988, which contemplates, among other things, a doubling of the EC's structural (agricultural, social, and regional) funds from 1988 to 1993 to support the reform of depressed areas in much of agricultural Spain and Portugal, must be seen as a partial response to Felipe Gonzalez's "conditions" necessary for the Southern European countries to give their green light to the "1992 Programme."[39]

Two of the Portuguese experts interviewed explained that their country's concern with the EC has to do mainly with those aspects relevant to the economic development of Portugal itself. This line of thinking has been confirmed by the victory in the last general elections of Cavaco Silva, a technocrat who would like to lower Portugal's already low foreign policy profile. The lack of Spanish experience in foreign affairs and of Portuguese economic resources are mentioned as short-run limitations of the new entrants' ability to act in Brussels. Last but not least, all those interviewed agree that a running period in the Community is needed before the Iberian countries are able to have any real influence on EC decisionmaking.[40] This may explain why, three years after their accession into the Community, their input into the shaping of EC external policies has been negligible (except regarding Latin America, as explained below).

To sum up, it seems that the Enlargement from the Ten to the Twelve and the completion of the EC's Internal Market will keep the Community busy with domestic matters for the forseeable future. Although the Spaniards and Portuguese interviewed agree with this assessment, they would like the Twelve to be more open to the world than the Ten—especially with regard to intensifying relations with ACP countries and extending them to the rest of the Third World, particularly to Latin America—but reluctantly admit that their countries will be most active in shaping domestic rather than external EC affairs.

4

Economic Policies Toward Other Areas of the World

Economic Interests vs. Foreign Policy Priorities

The press has written extensively on the expected input of Spanish decisionmakers in designing future European Community relations with Latin America. However, much less has been said about the policies, views, and intentions of Spain insofar as other regions of the world are concerned. Moreover, Portugal's role in the shaping of EC foreign policies has been totally neglected. Thus, in dealing with future EC policies toward specific regions, we will begin by surveying the past policies of Spain and Portugal toward these regions, and then endeavor to assess what might happen when these policies are blended with the acquis communautaire.

It is of interest that the importance the new EC members have traditionally attached to specific regions when designing their foreign policies does not always coincide with the economic stakes in these same regions. Therefore, statistical information and analysis on where the two new EC members have important economic interests at stake is presented to complement the information presented in Tables 2.1 through 2.5.

Next we detail the ranking of various regions in the priorities of each new member's government and use this as a basis for analyzing past, present, and possible future policies toward these areas, making use of official declarations, agency news, and press reviews, as well as interviews with experts and with Spanish, Portuguese, and Community officials.

Finally, we assess similarities and dissimilarities in the two countries' policies regarding extra-EC issues in order to estimate the force that they might exert in the future on the reshaping of present European Community policies.

Indexes of Sensitivity Toward Different Geographic Areas

Among the ways of determining the degree to which a country is interested in or sensitive to relations with any other country are possession of a common language, culture or religion, or the existence of a common historical heritage. As pointed out in Chapter 2, trade figures and trade dependence levels are also useful indicators, along with energy dependence levels. Still other indexes of interaction with specific areas are data on tourism, transport, foreign investment, and migration flows. (For Spain, we have been able to obtain figures on all four of these indicators, but figures on Portuguese foreign investment and migration were unavailable.)

Tourism. Of the 47 million people who visited Spain in 1986, 40 million or 86% originated in Europe, 37.6 million or 80% from EC countries.

As may be seen in Table 4.1, EFTA countries provided the largest number of extra-EC visitors (5.27%), followed by the United States and Canada (almost 2%). Thus, contrary to the impression that one might get from reading the press, tourism from Latin America and the Gulf countries is insignificant, at least in quantitative terms. The only Third World country with significant tourism to Spain is Morocco, but this is mostly due to the presence of Moroccan emigrants in Europe, who generally spend several hours or days in Spain on their way back to Morocco to visit their families.

Statistics of "arrivals of foreign visitors at frontiers" published by the OECD for Portugal show that 94.3% of its almost 10 million tourists in 1984 originated in Europe, more than 9 million or 91.1% from EC countries. Table 4.2 lists the non-EC countries that provided 6.8% of the 9% which came from nonmembers.

What was said of Spain can be repeated in the case of Portugal, except here the EC share is even larger than for Spain, because so many Spaniards vacation in Portugal. As might be expected, Moroccan tourism to Portugal is insignificant. What is striking is that, in view of Portugal's much-publicized links with its former colonies, there is not more tourism from these countries.

Transport and communication. International air links are a basic component of the communication infrastructure that help

Table 4.1
Tourism to Spain from Non-EC Countries (1986)

Percentages of Total Visitors

Morocco	5.16	Austria	0.55
Switzerland	1.94	Canada	0.37
U.S.	1.62	Argentina	0.33
Sweden	1.31	Japan	0.26
Norway	0.89	Brazil	0.21
Finland	0.58	Mexico	0.19

Source: Anuario *El Pais* 1987

Table 4.2
Tourism to Portugal from Non-EC Countries (1984)

Percentage of Total Visitors

United States	2.1	Switzerland	0.5
Latin America	1.1	Norway	0.3
Africa	0.9	Austria	0.2
Sweden	0.7	Finland	0.2
Canada	0.6	Japan	0.2

Source: OECD

maintain and develop trade and financial flows. Thus, in Tables 4.3 and 4.4 we present the number of flights per week from nonmember countries as a rough indication of how the EC's capacity to relate to other parts of the world changed when Spain and Portugal became members.

Twenty nonmember countries were selected for study on the basis of their relevance to the subject under analysis. To prevent double counting, only the country where the flight originated and the country where it finished was considered, that is, stopovers were excluded. A perusal of Tables 4.3 and 4.4 leads to three main observations: (1) Of all the countries surveyed, Brazil's air links with the Twelve show the largest increase over those with the Ten, followed by Argentina, Morocco, Mexico, Jordan, and Algeria. Clearly, then, links with Latin America are much more affected by the Enlargement than those with Mediterranean or EFTA countries. (2) Air links with Latin America and Morocco now represent a larger share of total extra-EC air links than before, to the detriment of other areas of the world not included in this survey because of their lesser relevance. (3) In terms of

Table 4.3
Number of Scheduled Airline Flights from Non-EC Countries per Week
(January 1987)

	EC-10	Spain	Portugal	EC-12	Rest of World	Total
Algeria	120	16	0	136	56	192
Morocco	90	19	3	112	52	164
Tunisia	84	4	0	88	41	129
Maghreb	294	39	3	336	149	485
Egypt	78	4	0	82	219	301
Jordan	20	2	1	23	69	92
Lebanon	20	1	0	21	52	73
Syria	13	0	0	13	57	70
Mashrek	131	7	1	139	397	536
Cyprus	34	0	0	34	46	80
Israel	91	4	1	96	70	166
Malta	43	0	0	43	19	62
Turkey	105	4	0	109	102	211
Yugoslavia	65	2	0	67	84	151
Total Med. Non-members	763	56	5	824	867	1,691
Austria	238	9	0	247	137	384
Finland	93	1	1	95	130	225
Norway	218	0	0	218	172	390
Sweden	164	7	0	171	137	308
Switzerland	909	67	21	997	395	1,392
EFTA[a]	1,622	84	22	1,728	971	2,699
Argentina	22	8	1	31	220	251
Brazil	20	5	8	33	139	172
Mexico	17	4	0	21	481	502

Source: *ABC World Airways Guides*, January 1987.
[a]Iceland not included

interdependence levels with the enlarged EC, while Malta, Switzerland, Tunisia, and Algeria still lead in terms of air links with the Twelve, Algeria has jumped from fourth to second place (after Switzerland), and Morocco has joined the leaders with the other EFTA countries (except for Finland), Israel, and Turkey following. Observe that, even after the Enlargement, Mashrek countries and Latin America are still much less dependent on air links with the Community.

Investments. With regard to investments, a distinction must be made between the foreign investment of the new EC members and the investments of foreigners in Spain or Portugal. Tables 4.5 and 4.6 show the geographical distribution of Spain's direct

Table 4.4
Percentage of Scheduled Airline Flights per Week to the EC
of All Flights from Non-EC Countries (January 1987)

	EC-10	EC-12	% Increase
Algeria	62.50	70.83	13.33
Morocco	54.88	68.29	24.44
Tunisia	65.12	68.22	4.76
Maghreb	60.62	69.28	14.29
Egypt	25.91	27.24	5.13
Jordan	21.74	25.00	15.00
Lebanon	27.40	28.77	5.00
Syria	18.57	18.57	0.00
Mashrek	24.44	25.93	6.11
Cyprus	42.50	42.50	0.00
Israel	54.82	57.83	5.49
Malta	69.35	69.35	0.00
Turkey	49.76	51.66	3.81
Yugoslavia	43.05	44.37	3.08
Total med: Non-members	45.12	48.73	7.99
Austria	61.98	64.32	3.78
Finland	41.33	42.22	2.15
Norway	55.90	55.90	0.00
Sweden	53.25	55.52	4.27
Switzerland	65.30	71.62	9.68
EFTA[a]	60.10	64.02	6.54
Argentina	8.76	12.35	40.91
Brazil	11.63	19.19	65.00
Mexico	3.39	4.18	23.53

Source: ABC World Airways Guides, January 1987.
[a]Iceland not included

Table 4.5
Recipients of Spain's Direct Foreign
Investment by Percentage (1986)[a]

EC	49.07	Panama	2.11
United States	19.79	Mexico	1.55
Chili	5.09	Cayman Islands	1.35
Bahamas	3.84	Argentina	1.19
Puerto Rico	3.63	Venezuela	1.11
Liechtenstein	3.25	Switzerland	0.80
Uruguay	2.38	Guatemala	0.72
		Liberia	0.67

Source: Boletín ICE, No. 2074, March 2–8, 1987.
[a]Countries receiving less than 0.5% of Spanish direct
investment have not been included

Table 4.6
Foreign Investment in Spain as a
Percentage of Total Foreign
Investment (1986)[a]

EC	64.53
United States	8.00
Canada	5.96
Switzerland/Liechtenstein	5.27
Dutch Antilles	7.89
Japan	2.47
Panama	1.83
Sweden	1.01

Source: Boletín ICE, No. 2071,
February 9–15 1987.
[a]Countries whose direct
investment in Spain is less than
0.5% of total foreign investment
have not been included

foreign investment and the geographical origin of investment in Spain, respectively, for the year 1986.

These two tables reveal: (1) After intra-EC investments, the United States is Spain's most important partner from the developed world, with Switzerland following the United States in terms of investment in Spain. (2) Latin American countries like Chile, Puerto Rico, Uruguay, Mexico, Argentina, and Venezuela receive a remarkably high percentage (14.95%) of total Spanish foreign investment (leaving aside tax havens) considering the present debt crisis ravaging Latin America.[41] (3) The list of Spain's significant investment partners contains no Arab or Mediterranean countries; authorized investments from oil exporting countries (including Venezuela) account for only 2% of total foreign investment in Spain in 1985 (down from 4.2% in 1983 and 8.6% in 1984). Only 0.29% of Spain's direct foreign investment in other countries went to oil exporting countries in 1986, dropping from 1.93% in 1985 and from a high of 8.45% in 1984. These trends are, of course, in line with the sharp reduction in the price of crude oil in recent years.

Emigrants. According to the Spanish National Institute of Emigration, 1,760,859 Spaniards were living outside Spain in 1986. Data showing the numbers of Spaniards residing in foreign countries and the percentage for each country are presented in Table 4.7.

After the EC and Switzerland, it is clear that the preferred

Table 4.7
Spaniards Residing Outside Spain (1986)[a]

	Number	% of Total
EC	638,185	36.00
Argentina	373,984	21.12
Venezuela	144,505	8.21
Brazil	118,567	6.73
Switzerland	108,352	6.16
United States	73,735	4.18
Uruguay	65,000	3.69
Canada	36,691	2.08
Mexico	30,045	1.70
Chile	30,000	1.70
Australia	22,500	1.27
Columbia	19,621	1.11

Source: Spanish National Institute of Emigration, 1987.
[a]Countries absorbing less than 1% of Spanish nationals have not been included

destination of Spanish emigrants is Latin America (53.8% of the total, including countries not in the table because they represent less than 1% of the grand total). The presence of Spanish nationals in Asia, Africa, and the Middle East is negligible.

The material on Portuguese ex-patriots is not complete. From what is available, it appears that more than one million Portuguese are currently living in France, and more than 600,000 in South Africa. Other countries with large numbers of Portuguese nationals are Angola, Argentina, Brazil, Macao, Morocco, Mozambique, Venezuela, and Zaire.

The countries that the Spanish people choose to emigrate to and invest in are not the same ones with which Spain has the largest trade dependence. In terms of Spanish migration and investment flows, Latin America, Switzerland, and the United States emerge as the key partner areas outside the EC, but a larger share of Spanish foreign trade is conducted with Mediterranean and Middle Eastern countries than with Latin America or EFTA countries (including Switzerland). This asymmetry must be taken into account when assessing the geographical areas in which one can expect Spain to be active within the framework of the EC.

The figures for emigration and trade dependence are also reflected in the mixed air link indicator, which relates simultaneously to trade in goods, services, and manpower. For instance, although Spain's air links with Morocco, Algeria, and Switzerland appear to be much more intense than those with Latin America, these figures have to be adjusted to take the much higher capacity of planes used in transatlantic travel into account. Even without this adjustment, there are more flights to Spain from Argentina than from Sweden, Norway, Finland, Tunisia, Israel, or any of the Mashrek countries. Moreover, there are also more flights to Portugal from Brazil than from any of the Mediterranean or EFTA countries, except for Switzerland.

Latin America and the Enlarged EC[42]

In this section we shall endeavor to assess several aspects of the Iberian countries' economic relations with Latin America, noting the similarities and differences between the two.

1. The Importance of Latin America in the New Members' Systems of Foreign Relations

All Spanish experts or officials who deal with foreign relations assert that, after Europe, Latin America is the most important area of action for Spanish diplomacy.[43] And there is a consensus on this among all of Spain's political parties, as evidenced by the 1978 Constitution, in which special mention is made of these two priorities. Thus, Article 56.1 of Title II of the Constitution, which refers to the Spanish Monarchy, states that:

> As Chief of State and the symbol of its unity and permanence, the King shall moderate the regular functioning of its institutions and assume the highest representation of the Spanish State in international relations, *particularly with the nations of its historical community.* . . .[44]

The reference here to "its historical community" clearly refers to both Europe and Latin America. With regard to the latter, Spain's cultural, linguistic, religious, and kinship relations with its former colonies are clearly self-explanatory. Moreover, proof of the importance Spain attaches to Latin America may be found in its special secretariat of state for International Cooperation and for Iberoamerica, created in August 1985, as one of the three divisions of the Spanish Foreign Ministry, alongside the secretariat of state for the European

Communities and the general secretariat of foreign policy. Finally, according to informed sources, Spain's embassies in every Latin American country are well endowed with human resources (although slightly less so in financial terms), in contrast with its embassies in other countries outside Europe.

In economic terms, however, Spain's interest and involvement with Latin America does not seem very different from those of the average EC member. For example, it is surprising that only 22.6% of Spain's direct foreign investment ended up in Latin America in 1985, even though this does represent a large jump from the 10.92% of 1984.[45] Trade with Latin America has been less intensive in recent years due to the debt crisis,[46] the decrease in the price of crude oil, and the prospects of entry into the EC; this has had the effect of reducing Spanish direct investment in Latin America from the more than 50% of total foreign investment that it represented in the mid-1970s. In this respect, Spaniards are as frightened as everyone else of the Latin American debt, because the southern hemisphere owed Spain more than $10 billion in 1986, or about 25% of the total foreign risk assumed by Spanish banks and their subsidiaries abroad. Moreover, taking into account the very low share of ODA in Spanish GNP, as indicated above, the fact that only 30% of the credit distributed at special terms by Spain's Development Aid Fund (average 1977–1983) was directed to Latin America is not very impressive. And trade with Central America, a subregion for which Spain feels special responsibility, has also been insignificant, representing a mere 0.42% of total exports and 0.23% of total imports in 1985.

Some Latin Americans contend that the change in Spanish economic policy toward them occurred the day that Spain opted for entry into the Community in 1977. But this argument is strongly rejected by the Spanish government of then and now. For instance, in 1979, the then Prime Minister Suárez stated in his program presented to the Senate that Spain's integration in Europe was perfectly compatible with Spain's Iberoamerican identity.[47] Similarly, in 1984, former Foreign Minister Morán stated that Spain's EC membership was generally supported by Latin American countries and that Spain would never had considered joining the EC if it did not think that it would greatly benefit Latin America.[48] While other Spanish officials did admit that during the difficult negotiations for accession into the EC, the Community would take precedence in the distribution of the government's time and resources, they felt that this would only be a temporary phenomenon that would be corrected after Spain's actual entry. Yet another argument in defense of the Spanish record in favor of Latin America made reference to Spain's discreetly favoring Latin American suppliers over other competitors over the years with regard to cereal and other basic food imports channelled through state trading agencies, and that this had allowed "high politics" to play a role in the distribution of import contracts in a way that benefited Latin America. However, Spanish officials accepted the fact that this could not continue after Spain's entry into the Community. Finally, active or passive Spanish participation in, or cooperation with, Latin American institutions like ECLA (Economic Commission for Latin America), the Andean Group, SELA (Sistema Economico Latino-Americano), and the Inter-American Development Bank is further proof of Spain's interest in and sensitivity toward Latin American economic problems.

For Portugal, while Latin America as a whole seems to hold third or fourth place in its foreign policy—after Europe, Portuguese-speaking Africa, and the U.S.—for obvious reasons there exists a sharp distinction between Brazil and the rest of Latin America. Portuguese experts do, however, insist that there is a totally different relationship between Portugal and Brazil, as compared with Spain and its former colonies. Brazilians, they say, do not have ambivalent feelings toward Portugal because they view their country as an overseas extension of Portugal in which the mother country and the ex-colony take turns at playing "big brother."

2. Spanish and Portuguese Views of Their Roles in EC-Latin American Relations

There is a sharp distinction between the two new EC members in this regard. Until the early 1980s, Spanish officials toyed with the idea that their country could act as a bridge between Europe and Latin America. However, the active disagreement with this thesis on the part of Latin American countries dispelled any illusions that Spain might have had. And, indeed, it was a naive idea, since the former colonies felt no need for a mediator.[49] Moreover, the Portuguese tended to reject such a role for themselves. To them, if any country is to be a bridge to Europe, it should be Brazil, the largest and most powerful nation in Latin America.

Gradually, the bridge theory was replaced by one in which

Spain is viewed as an "activating factor" in EC-Latin American relations or as a spokesperson for Latin America.[50] For, in the opinion of the Spanish government, relations between Latin America and Europe will have to develop. As Prime Minister Gonzalez has repeatedly stressed, Latin America shares the same Western culture as all of Europe and not only of Spain and Portugal, as has been erroneously believed. (This is not the case with ACP countries or with former colonies in Asia or the Arab world.) Moreover, Spain feels that its (successful) experience in making the transition from dictatorship to democracy renders it especially sensitive to the processes now going on in Latin American countries which have or are on the verge of adopting democratic regimes and values. Gonzalez maintains that Europe, as the birthplace of democracy, must support and promote this trend. It is Spain's contention that the two subcontinents share a common heritage, which deserves institutionalization and demands more communication.[51] Finally, Latin American countries have recently been requesting Spain's mediation in the U.N. when conflicts with the United States arise.[52]

Although all the above has to do with the political approach to relations between the EC and Latin America—especially because Spain's governing party (the PSOE) has made it clear that it does not view its role of "spokesperson" as including the negotiation of trade agreements with the Community on behalf of Latin America[53]—Spain, some officials say, will have to do something for that continent if it does not want to remain a third-rate power. For it is understood in Spain that Latin America is the one area of the world where it can exert a large measure of influence, certainly larger than it can in the Mediterranean. Thus, Spanish officials stress that the country will continue to maintain cordial dialogues with all political regimes in the subcontinent (including those of Cuba, Nicaragua, and Chile), in an effort to retain every bit of political capital it has garnered over the years. Independently of the EC, and since the early 1980s, Spain has been engaged in two large projects relating to Latin America: the celebration of the fifth century of the Discovery of America, in 1992, and a long-range plan for creating an "Iberoamerican Community of Nations," which would probably be similar to the Commonwealth, with its heavy emphasis on language and culture.

As far as Portugal is concerned, it has neither the human nor the financial means to be active in Latin America on any similar scale.

3. The Past and Present Contribution of the Two New Entrants to the Development of EC-Latin American Relations

It should be pointed out that, when Spanish experts ascribe an activating role to Spain in the context of present EC-Latin American relations, what they are in fact saying is that Spain may play an accelerating role in a process that was already underway in the EC. For there is a general consensus that the Falklands (or Malvinas) war of 1982 had the unexpected effect of putting back on the agenda relations that had been in crisis for many years. Of course—as explained by Leo Tindemans in early 1987, when he took over as president of the EC Council of Ministers—Spain's presence in the EC has contributed to the further development of the EC's special awareness toward South and Central America.[54] One official of the EC Commission, who describes Spain's attitude toward Latin America as more a question of tender affection than of business and trade, also uses the comparison of that between Britain and the Commonwealth: when Australia or New Zealand are the subject of Commission or Council discussions, British officials always side with their former colonies, even when they are not absolutely clear what they are voting for.

Spanish efforts to develop sensitivity toward Latin America can be traced back to the long period of negotiations for accession into the EC, when Spain tried to obtain the same treatment for Latin America as the ACP countries were getting. While this proved to be an impossible mission, for many reasons explained below, Spain did manage to include a Joint Declaration of Intent and its own unilateral declaration in the Accession Treaty of Spain and Portugal. The first of these documents "reaffirms [the EC's] resolve to extend and strengthen its economic, commercial and cooperation relations with [Latin American] countries," and states that the EC is prepared to step up relationships with the subcontinent, taking into account "the scope of the generalized system of preferences and the application of the economic cooperation agreements concluded or to be concluded with certain Latin American countries or groups of countries." Spain's unilateral declaration states that "in order to avoid sudden disturbances in its imports originating in Latin America, [it] has highlighted in the negotiations the problems arising from application of the acquis communautaire to certain products. In this respect, partial and temporary solutions have [so far] been adopted for tobacco, cocoa and coffee." Moreover,

"Spain . . . proposes to find permanent solutions in the context of the Generalized System of Preferences, when that is next revised, or in the context of other existing Community mechanisms."

One of the results of the Joint Declaration was the European Council's decision at The Hague on June 27, 1986—following a Spanish suggestion—to ask the Commission to draw up a new proposal concerning relations with Latin America. This resulted in a December 1986 Commission communication to the Council of Ministers, known as the Cheysson Document,[55] in which several new ideas regarding Latin America were put forth: an increase in aid to its relatively less developed countries; an improvement in the Community's GSP to benefit its least developed countries; and encouraging new regional integration schemes by providing incentives such as accumulation of rules of origin. Although most of these proposals were adopted by the Council on June 22, 1987, to the dismay of many in Spain, there has not yet been any talk of concluding preferential trade agreements between the EC and South American countries, or of according Latin American exports special treatment. Moreover, the Council resolution did not even specify how the proposals that were accepted will be financed. Thus, in the opinion of those in charge in Spain, the document does not go far enough. However, most of them do agree that it was the best they could get, for they are now aware that the Lomé Convention represents the continuation of pre-existing relationships between newly independent countries and their former mother countries, and that this special relationship cannot be reproduced elsewhere.

Not only is the Community not prepared to give Latin American imports any special tariff preferences, it is also unwilling to consider any sort of compensatory financing to stabilize revenues deriving from commodities exported by Latin America. In this respect, in 1986, Spain tried in vain to have COMPEX facilities that had been offered currently to least developed countries that are not partners to the Lomé Convention extended to some Central American countries.[56]

In yet another domain, Spain succeeded, after two years of pressuring hard for it, in having the Community's budget for "Technical and financial cooperation with nonassociated countries in Asia and Latin America" separated so that the two geographical areas can be distinguished. But the change, introduced in early 1988, is more symbolic than anything else.

With regard to the many developments concerning local conflicts in Central America, Spain has been very active in the context of EPC. And, although we are only dealing with political subjects insofar as they are relevant to external economic relations, members of the Spanish Socialist party insist that the Spanish political contribution should not be underrated by Latin Americans merely because Spain has not yet been able to achieve better results in the economic field.[57] Spain's efforts in this area have resulted in, for example, the institutionalization of the dialogue between the EC and Central America, after the three San José meetings that began taking place in 1984. Meanwhile two additional conferences took place, one in Hamburg in 1988 ("San José IV") and one in San Pedro Sula in 1989 ("San José V"). Moreover, a Cooperation Agreement between the European Community and the signatories of the General Treaty on Central American Economic Integration and Panama was agreed to on November 12, 1985, providing, among others things, for the creation of a Joint Cooperation Committee.[58] Nonetheless, many question such agreements on the basis that they are merely declaratory on the part of the EC, and do not mean much in economic terms. Nor do these officials believe that it is fair for the EC to demand that Central America improve human rights as a condition for talking about anything else when the same rule is not applied to ACP countries.[59]

To sum up, as of mid 1989, the Spanish input in EC-decisionmaking vis-a-vis Latin America has been more in the domain of "atmospherics" and consciousness raising than in operational matters. Taking the generally prolonged EC decisionmaking process into account, however, their modest record to date has only shown the Spaniards that they will need much patience in order to change things in this area.

Portugal, on the other hand, has not expended much effort on Latin American matters and, according to some sources, views with caution Spain's exertions to have the EC deal with the subject. Portugal is interested in seeing that there is a distinction made between Brazil, an economic giant with particular problems, and the rest of Latin America, where the United States is omnipresent, particularly in Central America. Not only does Portugal think that the EC must respect the sensitivities of the United States in this area of the world, but Portuguese officials think that the Latin Americans should approach the Community, not the other way around.

4. Spain's Possible Future Contribution
Toward Improved EC-Latin American Relations

The two fields of the economic sphere in which the European Community has the potential of affecting relationships with non-members are development assistance and trade. In regard to assistance, there seems to be little that Spain will be able to do in the relatively near future. To begin with, most of the EC aid funds currently budgeted for are tied to conventions or Agreements with countries in other areas of the world. And there is little short-term hope that the credit envelopes for overseas aid will be increased because of the net cost of the last Enlargement. For this not only necessitates extra costs involved in sustaining the incomes of the farmers among the newcomers, mostly by price supports, but also involves the costs surrounding the Integrated Mediterranean Programs—through which the economies of the Mediterranean regions of France, Greece, and Italy are to be restructured. Moreover, because Portugal has a similar or lower per capita GNP than Argentina, Venezuela, or Panama—and one that is not much higher than those of Mexico, Uruguay, and Brazil—it is likely that it will strongly object to any across-the-board aid increases. Thus, the only assistance to which the EC is likely to agree is that to the extremely poor countries in Central America. In this connection, as may be seen in Table 4.8, some Caribbean countries have higher per capita incomes than that of Portugal, Greece, or Spain!

If Spain is committed to convincing other EC members to accept the moral obligation of contributing to new EC development funds or to allow funds to be deviated from the regular EC budget for that purpose, it must provide an example by considerably boosting its own bilateral aid levels, including those directed to Latin America. As explained above, Spain expects to reach the OECD's average record of ODA as a percentage of GNP (0.36%) by 1992.

On the other hand, from now on, Spain may try to influence the distribution of untied credit by the European Investment Bank (EIB) to favor Latin America. As a matter of fact, EIB credit does not necessarily have to be directed to specific development projects—resulting in a wide margin of maneuver (i.e., usage of funds for adjustment assistance). Another possibility might be for Spain to try to persuade the EC to include some of the poor Central American countries as beneficiaries of the EDF or to extend some of the advantages offered to ACP countries to them.

Table 4.8
Per Capita Income (1986, in dollars)

Bermuda	20,410
Trinidad and Tobago	5,360
Puerto Rico	5,190
Barbados	5,140
Spain	4,860
Greece	4,000
Venezuela	3,580
Portugal	2,370
Argentina	2,360
Panama	2,180
Uruguay	1,920
Mexico	1,900
Brazil	1,830

Source: The World Bank Atlas, 1988.

This has already been brought up in the case of the Dominican Republic, but has met with stiff resistance from other EC members, as well as from ACP countries, on the basis that this might encourage other Latin American countries to request similar treatment. There is now, however, clear indications that—under relentless pressure by Spain—the Dominican Republic, together with Haiti and Namibia, may be the first Spanish-speaking country to become a cosignatory of the next EC-ACP Convention due in 1990.

In the area of trade, Spain has had to abandon any hope of obtaining the accession of Latin American countries to the present Lomé Convention or to the one being currently negotiated, or to have the EC sign a similar convention with them. This is not only due to obstacles from other EC members, but to lack of interest on the part of the Latin American countries as well, because those most affected by the Iberian countries' accession to the EC are among the more developed countries in the Southern Cone.[60]

Spain's unremitting pressure might either delay the future elimination of certain Latin American Newly Industrializing Countries (NICs) from the list of GSP beneficiaries,[61] or might result in some improvement in the scheme that would favor those countries in Latin America. Spanish action might also prevent a further erosion in the value of the GSP derived from fresh concessions given to ACP or Mediterranean countries. But other EC members will not fail to remind Spain that NICs must all eventually be graduated into the category of developed countries.

In this respect, it is not clear how the Community or the Latin American countries themselves would respond to a proposal by Spain that the latter be treated similarly to Israel or Turkey. This would involve the conclusion of bilateral agreements (e.g., between the EC and Brazil) that would lead to the creation in the very long term of industrial free trade areas based upon a measure of reciprocity. Such a strategy makes particular sense for countries that have reached a stage of development that allows them to liberalize imports from developed countries progressively. Moreover, this would go a long way toward reducing trade dependence on the United States, which is so much desired by Latin Americans. It remains to be seen how the United States would react to such a proposal.

Spain's first real opportunity to show leadership has only just begun in the first semester of 1989, when it acceded to the presidency of the Council of Ministers in January 1989. Spain has decided to place EC relations with Latin America as a top priority for action during its term in the presidency, with a strong emphasis on relations with Central America. Spain feels that progress with regard to this subregion would be easier to obtain, since its relations with the EC are already better structured than those of other areas in Latin America, and that there exists the real possibility of carrying out an ambitious project in a relatively short time.

Stressing the need to develop intraregional trade in Central America, the countries of the region, with the backing of the Spanish presidency, proposed in San Pedro Sula in February 1989 (a meeting known as San José V) to implement the above-mentioned objective by means of EC financial support to a regional system of payments. The idea was accepted in principle by the EC's Council of Ministers, which gave the green light to begin working on the project for subsequent approval in late 1989 under the French presidency. This demonstrates a measure of realism from the Spanish government of what was feasible. Other ideas were submitted during the same meeting, such as the need for specific support for the least developed countries in Central America, such as Nicaragua and Honduras, in the form of a fund for export promotion to be supported by the EC. This latter project is not likely to be approved before 1990, while a third project proposing EC member states participation in the expansion of the capital base of the Central American Bank for Economic Integration was left for later discussion.

On the other hand, Spain sought in the early months of 1989 to discuss debt problems in the context of the Community, but not with much success. On this matter it encountered strong resistance from many other EC members, particularly the United Kingdom and the Federal Republic of Germany, who were not prepared to transfer debt responsibilities to the Community for fear of impairing their position in the International Monetary Fund, the World Bank, or the Club of Paris.

It should be noted that the fact that the present Spanish government's position on Latin America is supported by all parties in the political spectrum means that it can usually count on all Spanish votes in the European Parliament. This also implies that a change of government would not lead to deviations from the single-minded political line drawn by the present Socialist government. Also of note is the fact that the current "vacuum" in EC-Latin American relations offers disproportionately large possibilities for a strongly motivated member like Spain to step in. However, Spain is finding out that most Northern members of the European Community are increasingly less interested in what goes on in Central America and certainly view "rocking the boat" (as far as their relations with the United States are concerned) with caution. Thus, there does not seem to be any basis for having one common Latin American foreign policy for the whole Community.[62] Nor has the example of Greece proven encouraging for Spain in this respect, because the former's ambition to become the mediator between Europe and the Arab world has failed. Spanish government circles therefore tend to view Britain's role in European Political Cooperation as a model, rather than that of Greece. Readers will decide for themselves if this is a too optimistic a view of Spain's possible input into EC policies.[63]

The Mediterranean Dimension

Importance of Extra-European Mediterranean Countries in the Foreign Relations System of the Two New EC Members

As stated previously,[64] the Mediterranean dimension of the Enlargement should take precedence over the Latin American component for Spain, because of proximity and other highly strategic factors, which are absent in the case of the American continent, even though the latter may be closer to Spain culturally speaking. And, as shown in Tables 2.1 and 2.2, the trade interests at stake in the Mediterranean area are also more critical than those in Latin America. In other words, the pocket and the gun are not located where the heart lies.[65] Moreover, as shown in Tables 2.4 and 2.5, Spain's energy dependence on countries bordering the Mediterranean is very large by Community standards, and in terms of tourism, Moroccans alone account for a larger number of tourists to Spain than all of the Latin Americans. Spanish direct investment overseas is the only domain where Latin America is dominant, in comparison with the Mediterranean Basin. Finally, the Enlargement itself will only tend to increase the importance of the Mediterranean area to the Spanish economy, to the partial detriment of Latin America.

Although the Mediterranean officially ranks third in the order of priorities of Spanish diplomacy, by all accounts the resources devoted to this region by Spain's Ministry of Foreign Affairs are meager, especially since its entry into the European Community, which now absorbs a great deal more human and financial resources. Indeed, it seems that the Mediterranean would rank fourth or fifth instead of third if it were not for the fact that, as a Mediterranean country, Spain cannot ignore this conflictive area which can affect its territorial integrity and security.[66] In other words, in the eyes of Spaniards it is inevitable that they place the Mediterranean in third place, rather than lower down in priority. As J. Fuentes indicates in his interesting article,[67] danger, menace and even actual invasion has historically come from the south, rather than the north.[68] This opinion is shared by almost all Spanish experts. From the military and strategic viewpoints, it is the southern flank that must be given priority, since Spain and France are at peace (the Pyrenees form an impressive barrier in any case), and Spain is now a member of the Community. With respect to various countries in Northern Africa, however, Spain must act with caution, because several of them have taken positions that collide with what it considers cornerstones of its foreign policy. And, vis-a-vis North Africa, Spain defends three principles that have the potential of leading to open conflict or, theoretically, even to war: (1) Ceuta, Melilla, the Canary Islands, and the Balearic Islands are integral parts of the Spanish nation, not colonies; (2) Spain is a Western country; and (3) as a Western country, it has become a member of the EC and of NATO.

In terms of the first principle, all Maghreb countries

challenge Spain's rights to Ceuta and Melilla,[69] and Algeria has even supported, at times, a movement fighting for the independence of the Canary Islands. In reference to the third principle, both Algeria and Libya were against Spain's entering NATO, Libya even objected to its joining the EC.[70] All this disturbs the Spaniards. It is therefore not surprising that, as Fuentes puts it, the Arab world is not very highly regarded in Spain. He even goes so far as to assert that Spanish participation in NATO can be justified by the existence of a menace from the south. While this opinion would be rejected by many in the general public, most Spanish experts do recognize that the 14 km of the Strait of Gibraltar do not provide a very strong barrier between Northern Africa and Spain. In this connection, J. Descallar stresses that, unlike other European countries, Spain has an almost direct frontier with the Arab world.[71] Not surprisingly, people involved in defense matters define Spain's strategic space as situated between the Pyrenees, the Balearic Islands, the Atlas Mountains, and the Canary Islands. Obviously, Spain's incorporation into the EC brings the Community into closer geographical contact with the Arab countries and Africa. This has tremendous implications for the EC in view of the project of completing the Internal Market in 1992, a program envisioning among others things the free movement of labor inside the EC borders. This new reality might encourage potential migrants from North Africa to penetrate the huge EC labor market through neighboring Spain.

Beyond the possibility of a direct threat to Spanish territory, there is also the Spanish fear that the instability and turbulence in Northern Africa might spill over to Spain, in terms of political and non-political refugees or terrorism. In this respect, Islamic radicalism is perceived as a particularly dangerous threat to Spain, in the event that it spreads to countries in Northern Africa. Although rarely expressed, the fear here is that, as happened over a thousand years ago, Islam would again invade part of Spain. This prognostication is not altogether unrealistic in view of the demographic pressure building up in the Maghreb. For, the present population of Algeria and Morocco is 40 million, which is expected to reach the 60 million mark soon after the year 2000, while Spain's birthrate has dropped significantly in recent years. Thus, for many in Spain, the country's Arab past is taken as a warning. Others, however, view this in a much more positive manner. Those who are not frightened by North Africa tend to adopt the same line of thinking expounded by Franco and one of his foreign ministers, Fernando María Castiella, that precisely because of its past Spain is in a position to understand the Arabs much better than other European countries. Some even go as far as to point out the ethnic Arab component of the Spanish population. These same people also tend to view Spain as a potential mediator in inter-Arab or other Middle Eastern conflicts.

One Spanish official predicted that relations between the European Community and Mediterranean nonmembers will become less conflict-ridden because of Spain's EC membership. But there is no consensus regarding this point, as opinions on the Arab world are very disparate in Spain. Our own analysis reveals that, for the foreseeable future, the prevailing attitude toward the Arab world will be more one of anxiety and fear, than of sympathy.

For instance, a relatively new security concern is that along with France, the Maghreb countries might provide a nearby sanctuary for enemies of the Spanish state, such as the Euzkadi Ta Azkatasuna (ETA) terrorists, some of whom have been in Algeria for long periods or have received military training in different countries of Northern Africa.

In terms of *strategic* importance, however, a very sharp distinction must be drawn between the Maghreb (including Libya and Mauritania) and the rest of the Mediterranean and the Arab world. On the one hand, Spain has never been involved in Middle Eastern crises and never had colonies in the area. And on the other, Morocco is by far the Maghreb country that ranks first in Spanish minds, followed by Algeria. Spanish elites and government circles know these two countries well, and events that take place there are monitored closely. In addition, relations with these two Maghreb countries are relatively intense. Libya, Tunisia, and Mauritania follow, even though Spain's economic interests in Tunisia are very limited and that country is already being "taken care of" by France.[72]

It is in the economic component that Spanish officials make a less sharp distinction between the Western and Eastern Mediterranean. In this respect, Egypt and the Gulf countries are important trade and financial partners when compared, for example, to Tunisia or Mauritania which are much closer to home. Nonetheless, in economic terms, Algeria, Libya, and Morocco still play a primary role in Spanish diplomacy.[73] This explains why Spaniards tend to use "the Mediterranean," "Africa," "Northern Africa" and "the Maghreb" to refer essentially to the same area. It also explains why there has been on-going attention on the part of the Ministry of Foreign Affairs and the prime minister's office regarding ways to deal with what is seen as an area of conflict virtually on Spain's doorsteps. When Adolfo Suárez was Prime Minister (1976–1980), a "policy of equilibrium" was maintained between Algeria and Morocco because the problem of the formerly Spanish Sahara was still unsolved. Later on, the Socialist government switched to what it calls a global policy, although this does not differ much from the previous one, except, perhaps, that the present policy places more emphasis on development cooperation.

In the meantime, debt has become a "hot potato." For, Morocco owed Spain more than $400 million at the end of 1986,[74] while Spain was on the receiving end when the dispute over the fair price of Algerian gas that erupted between the two countries was settled in 1985. Not surprisingly, therefore, Morocco is seen as an economic liability, and Algeria as an asset.[75] Moreover, Spain competes with Morocco, but not with Algeria, for the same European fruit and vegetable markets, and has to contend with Morocco over other economically important items like Spanish fishing rights in Moroccan territorial waters and the right of passage for Moroccan agricultural exports to Europe over Spanish territory.

In spite of the fact that the other Iberian member of the Community, Portugal, is classified as a Mediterranean country by Northern and Central Europe, the Portuguese view themselves as an Atlantic entity. Although they are prepared to recognize the Latin input in their way of life, no Portuguese talks about his Arab past or about being able to understand the Arab mentality, as do Spaniards. Thus, one can say that Portugal is less sensitive to Mediterranean problems than Spain, even though strategically speaking, Portugal and Spain together dominate the entrance to the Mediterranean Basin, and as defined by one Portuguese expert consulted, Portugal shares a sea frontier with Morocco.

Being much further away from Morocco than Spain, Portugal does not view the former as a menace, even though it is near enough to transfer its domestic instability. Thus, like Spain, Portugal has an interest in strengthening or at least preserving the present pro-Western regime in Morocco. There are many bilateral agreements between the two countries, and they cooperate in military maneuvers. In fact, good relations with Morocco are seen by some in Portugal as a counterweight to Spain's presence in every aspect of Portuguese life as a consequence of both countries' entry into the Community.

Exactly what this means is still unclear. One interpretation is that Portugal would be happy to have Spain kept busy with Moroccan headaches for as long as possible. Another is that Portugal would be prepared to cooperate strategically with Spain only if a third country in the region such as Morocco is a partner to strategic cooperation.

Beyond Morocco, Portugal has no other direct strategic interests in the Mediterranean. Yet, because Portugal is a close ally of the United States, which does have many strategic interests in the Middle East and in Northern Africa, Portugal must be involved in the area at least indirectly.

In the economic field, the Mediterranean is several times less important to Portugal than to Spain (see Tables 2.1 and 2.2 for trade-related figures). Because fewer Portuguese fish in Moroccan waters, there is a lesser potential for conflict between the two countries over fishing rights. And competition with Morocco in EC markets is limited to only a few products—although, according to several persons consulted, this situation may change with the Enlargement. For, Portugal could become a large exporter of fruit and vegetables if EC structural funds and the whole protective CAP machinery became geared to that purpose. Finally, although Portugal is much less dependent than Spain on gas and crude oil from Libya and Algeria, the Middle Eastern countries provide a very high percentage of its total petroleum imports.

Spanish and Portuguese Views of Their Roles in EC-Mediterranean Relations

Surprising as it may seem in view of what is presented in the last section, neither Iberian country has given much thought to Mediterranean relations to date. Spanish officials and experts speak very candidly of the Mediterranean as Spain's "asignatura pendiente" (literally, "pending course"). But Prime Minister F. Gonzalez and King Juan Carlos have visited most North African countries since Spain entered the EC, which does evince some interest in the area. Moreover the Spanish government has included Maghreb countries among those slated to receive bilateral ODA on a permanent basis,[76] deciding, for example, in July 1988, to allocate to them a soft- and long-term credit package of 125 billion pesetas (about one billion dollars), to be used over a five-year period.[77]

On Middle Eastern affairs, caution is the rule. There is no

official record of Spain wishing to act as mediator, as is the case for Central America.[78] Nor is there any indication that it will take up the role of bridge to the Mediterranean despite the fact that many historians claim that the Iberian Peninsula has played such a role in the past. The most that Spain seems prepared to do is to provide a "balcony of the EC" from which to observe the Arab world. (Spanish views on the Euro-Arab dialogue are analyzed later on.)

As far as Portugal is concerned, it has exhibited no interest whatsoever in the area.

Spanish and Portuguese Efforts to Shape EC's Mediterranean Policy

A good starting point here is to point out that Spain was part of the EC's Mediterranean Policy since its inception in 1972, but opted out in 1973–1974, when it became clear that General Franco's rule was coming to an end and that membership in the EC was almost within reach. Until it opted out, Spain had been working discreetly with Israel in Brussels toward a revision of the 1970 Preferential Agreements with the Community that would take into account the effect of Britain's entry into the EC on the two countries. Negotiations were stalled in 1973, because of the Yom Kippur War, and in early 1974, Spain parted ways with Israel. Envisioning the day when Spain would be a full member of the Community and would benefit from the principles of CAP, including the Community's preference, Spain was no longer interested in revising the agreement, which had after all served its industry well.

Although this position has not changed since, it has been reshaped in several ways since Spain's entry into the Community. In general, the policy is to obtain new concessions from the Community that will not be extended to other Mediterranean countries. And if that is not possible, Spain will object to any concession that other EC members might wish to confer on nonmember Mediterranean countries. What is most important to Spain is that its agricultural products continue to receive preferential treatment over and above that received by Mediterranean nonmembers. This means that it has opted to promote agricultural exports by maximizing artificial trade diversion in its favor, something that is not always obvious from the official records. For instance, although it was agreed that, after a transition period, Spain was to receive full access into EC agricultural markets as compensation for its opening Spanish industrial markets to EC competition, it does not follow that, by this, Spain was trying to maximize trade creation. This is because there is a huge difference between the level of protectionism built into CAP and the degree to which Spain opened its economy prior to 1986. Average industrial tariffs in Spain were already much lower than the tariff-equivalent of CAP's nontariff barriers on fruit and vegetables imports by the Ten. Moreover, the Treaty of Accession of June 12, 1985, compelled Spain to adjust to a low average Common External Tariff, and to eliminate tariffs on imports not only from the EC but also from EFTA, ACP, and Mediterranean countries. Last, but not least, it had to adopt the EC's GSP scheme. All this implies that, as far as Spanish industrial imports are concerned, there is a lot of potential trade creation, and any negative trade diversion effects on third countries should be widely spread out. The reverse is not true for Spanish exports of fruit and vegetables, which by and large are not expected to displace exports from France and Italy, which would be trade creation, but rather those of Mediterranean nonmembers (i.e., trade diversion). Moreover, the negative effects are concentrated on only a few countries: Morocco, Israel, and Cyprus.

What would have seemed the most equitable solution would have been for Spain to ask to be compensated for the trade diversion in products originally imported from nonmember countries through favored access for its products into the Community (another trade diversion). For example, Spain could have claimed that, since CAP's regime for continental products would hurt its own consumers, because trade diversion in favor of France and against the United States would result in higher prices for the same products, Spain should be allowed to sell agricultural products to the Community that had previously been purchased from nonmembers.

Prior to Spain's accession into the EC, Spain had not realized that the source of its economic problem lay in the extortionate protectionism of CAP and therefore aligned itself with those countries striving to maintain or even enlarge it. For CAP was seen (as in France in the early days of the Community) as compensating the Customs Union with regard to industrial products. More recently, however, the Spanish public has learned from the press about the effects of trade diversion against the United States in cereals. And this has led to a reevaluation of the situation to focus on what Spanish officials should have accented in the first place. But even then, the line taken has been that EC Mediterranean countries should be granted the same protection for fruits and vegetables that Northern Europeans receive for the products of interest to them. In other words, the Spaniards have been operating under the combined assumptions that CAP as it is presently constituted is a given, and that agricultural protection should benefit all EC members equally. Alas, efficiency considerations are strangely absent from the whole approach.

The effects of this philosophy may be seen from what has happened between 1983 and 1988. At the end of 1983, the first round of negotiations between the Ten and Mediterranean nonmembers considered the possible effects of the Enlargement on the latter. This did not lead to a proposal from the Commission to the Council of Ministers until July 1985, so that a mandate was not given to the Commission until November 1985, or more than two years after the original negotiations—which was, of course, too late for the Ten to reach any agreement with Mediterranean nonmembers before Spain's entry into the Community. This delay, initiated by Italy with Spain's backing from the outside, succeeded despite the Commission's desire—supported by the UK and the Federal Republic of Germany—to formulate an agreement before 1986. Italy benefited from the delay because it meant that Spain and Portugal would be sitting in the Council to support the Italian policy of minimizing trade concessions to Mediterranean nonmembers when it came up for a vote. Both Spain and Italy also wanted to narrow the gap between these negotiations and those on renewal of the Second Financial Protocols attached to Cooperation and Free Trade Agreements with Mediterranean countries, which were expected to take place in mid-1986. They believed that linking the two events would put the onus on Northern EC members, the idea here being that beefing up the financial component of the Global Mediterranean Policy would oblige Northern members to shoulder some of the burden involved in compensating Mediterranean nonmember countries.

In March 1986, the Commission asked for an additional mandate. This led to a new compromise, proposed by the (Dutch) president of the Council of Ministers on April 17, 1986, which was vetoed by Spain. Before it would agree to the compromise, Spain wanted to make certain that Canary Island agriculture would be treated at least as well as that of nonmember Mediterranean countries.[79] Without entering into the ensuing negotiations between the EC and Spain, the latter's veto acted to block the development of the EC Mediterranean Policy until October 1986. In answer to Moroccan charges that Spain's actions were aimed at increasing instability in Northern Africa, Spain replied that it did not question the concessions included in the compromise of April 1986,[80] and that it only wanted to ensure that the Canary Islands would not suffer in comparison with third Mediterranean countries. The real aim, however, was to place the Canary Islands somewhere in between the Mediterranean countries and the Iberian Peninsula with regard to EC agricultural markets.[81] The bases of the Spanish government's position was its fear that it had already accepted too many conditions during the negotiations for accession and that this might lead to domestic political problems. It was in this light that the Spanish veto aimed at obtaining new concessions for Canary Island agriculture.[82] Ironically the reason why the Islands were excluded from CAP in the Accession Treaty was that the Canarian autonomous government had requested this several years earlier.

In any event, the compensation being offered by the EC to satisfy Spain's requests on Canary Island agriculture were not considered sufficient. According to unofficial sources, Spain wanted further compensation in the form of new fishing rights from France before it would withdraw its veto. And when this was agreed upon, Spanish Foreign Minister Fernandez Ordoñez, told the Moroccan authorities that a compromise had been reached. This opened the way for renewed negotiations with Mediterranean countries at the end of 1986, which resulted in agreements being signed by the parties involved (except for Morocco and Yugoslavia) some months later.[83] Here too, Spain linked its signing of these agreements to the conclusion of negotiations on the Technical Adaptation Protocol, the agreement outlining Spain and Portugal's adoption of the GMP Agreements. Thus, once again, there was a simultaneous signature and ratification of the two types of agreements by the European Parliament at the end of 1987 (except for the important cases of Morocco, for which procedures were completed in mid-1988, and Israel, for which the European Parliament did not ratify the protocols until October 1988 for political reasons).

Although Portugal's attitude toward the renewal of EC agreements with Mediterranean countries is close to that of Spain, it has kept a lower profile on the issue. As stated by the Portuguese Foreign Ministry in 1986,[84] Portugal's position has been to minimize EC concessions in sectors that might hurt

Portuguese interests (e.g., in the areas of tomato concentrate and textiles), to prevent any erosion of the Community's preference resulting from Commission recommendations to reduce reference prices on Moroccan tomato exports or Cypriot table grapes in the future, and to fight any increase in tariff quotas on potato imports from Cyprus.

It therefore seems that joint action by Italy, Spain and Portugal has had a substantial impact on the timing of agreements and quite an impact on the contents as well. But, what has been achieved so far pales in comparison with what this author found were Spain's initial intentions in the years preceding the Enlargement. At that time, Spain's clear-cut aim was to obtain the phasing out of fruit and vegetable exports of Mediterranean third countries to the Community over a period of ten years, an aim that was totally rejected by the Commission, which planned to maintain the Mediterranean countries' share in EC imports—an idea that was in turn rejected by Spain. The final compromise between the two sides—that only "traditional exports" would be preserved—meant that Mediterranean countries will have to forget about fostering economic development on the basis of increased agricultural exports to the EC. As is well documented in the literature, this is an alarming thought for developing countries such as Morocco, Turkey, Cyprus, Tunisia, and Egypt, but less so for Israel or Yugoslavia.[85]

Moreover at the end of 1985, both Spain and Portugal planned to link the trade negotiations between the EC and Mediterranean countries with the renewal of the Second Financial Protocols. Both countries wanted an increase of 70% over and above what was distributed in the previous protocol,[86] while the UK, Germany, Denmark, and the Netherlands wanted a much less significant increase. In its proposal to the Council, the Commission acceded to the Southern European countries' requests, but the Belgian president sought a compromise that led to a final average increase of 59% in early 1987. This meant that Egypt and Morocco obtained above average rates of increase (+63%), a decision in which Spain and Portugal obviously played a role.

Between spring 1987 and early 1988, two additional conflicts involving the EC, Spain, and Morocco exploded, both of which illustrate further the problematic relations between the latter two countries. The first had to do with the 1983 fishing agreement between Spain and Morocco which was to lapse by August 1, 1987.

Because Spain was now a member of the Community, it was the EC that had to negotiate a new agreement. Although it was decided to extend the previous agreement for an additional five months after substantial debate, unofficial sources report that Morocco tried to link the issue to the still uncompleted negotiations with the Twelve for renewal of the 1976 Cooperation Agreement. However, it soon became apparent that the financial benefits being offered to Morocco were unsatisfactory, and that Morocco expected Spain to offer compensation on a bilateral basis. Spain countered by offering, among others things, to open negotiations on overland traffic rights for Moroccan agricultural produce as of October 1987, something which had been previously denied due to opposition from Spanish citrus growers. These negotiations, which were not concluded until March 1988, provided for a transition period to run from November 1988 to January 1996, during which transportation quotas are being progressively enlarged, to reach complete liberalization by the end of the period.[87] Here it should be noted that this was not a real concession on Spain's part, since the Treaty of Rome obliges Spain to grant traffic rights to Morocco. As for renegotiations of the fishing agreement, tension reached a high in winter of 1988, when Morocco refused to allow Spanish trawlers to fish in Moroccan territorial waters because the Community was unwilling to accept certain of Morocco's conditions.[88] Eventually, both partners agreed that the Community would pay much higher dues than those paid by Spain, and that there would be a 20% reduction in the amount of fish caught by the Community in Moroccan waters (including those facing ex-Spanish Sahara), over a four-year period. This must be considered somewhat of a blow to Andalusian and Canary Islands fisheries.

Beyond these episodes, however, there is the question as to the long-range intentions of the two new EC members.

Spanish and Portuguese Plans for Shaping EC Relations with Mediterranean Nonmember Countries

One of the most unexpected results of the Southern Enlargement of the EC is that stabilization of three new Northern Mediterranean democracies (namely, Spain, Greece, and Portugal) is being obtained partially at the expense of the economic stability of Southern and Eastern Mediterranean nonmembers. Another is that this burden is being imposed on

Third World countries that have become closer neighbors of the Community with Spain's entry. This means that the EC must become more rather than less open to their plight, not for altruistic reasons, but because it must worry about preserving itself, as European political cooperation is still in its infancy. One only has to consider what an invasion of Ceuta and Melilla by Morocco would imply for the Community itself. Paradoxically, the last Enlargement has reduced the Community's ability to maneuver in the Mediterranean. This is not only because, after the transition period, Spain's agricultural potential will be unleashed, which will pose problems to other Mediterranean exporters of fruit, vegetables, and olive oil to EC markets, but also because EC self-sufficiency will have been attained in many sectors. This means loss of markets for nonmembers both within the EC and in other third markets. At that stage, the United States and Brazil will also be affected, and the Community will be pressured to step in with something other than trade concessions if it does not want to lose its influence in the Mediterranean area.

One possibility could be massive development assistance. Now that the United States is restraining ODA, there may be a role for the EC in this domain. One should consider Shimon Peres's proposals for a "Marshall Plan" in the Middle East in this context. It is true that the EC has not been doing as much as it could in terms of development finance. Spain and Portugal would agree that the EC should do more in this area. After all, the Community devotes a mere 0.6% of its total annual expenditure to nonmember Mediterranean states.[89] Moreover the Community's share of net public assistance to these countries between 1979 and 1983 represented 2% of the foreign assistance total—as compared with 31% from the United States. Even more interesting is the fact that, between 1981 and 1983, these countries' share of total U.S. aid to the Third World was 37.2%, whereas their share of Community aid was 11.6%, and of the member states' bilateral aid, only 8.6%.

Thus, the Community is taking a back seat in the Mediterranean at a time when logic or prudence would suggest that more involvement is necessary. The EC's relative withdrawal is even more marked in regard to the Eastern Mediterranean, a trend that will only continue to be reinforced by the Enlargement. Although foreign ministry officials in Spain keep repeating that they want the Maghreb to be anchored to Europe, sometimes even extending this to other Northern African

countries, when they are asked what Spain thinks the EC should
do to acomplish this, their answers are less clear-cut: promotion
of scientific and technical cooperation or financial help to
promote the diversification of the African economies are vaguely
mentioned. (Portuguese officials, when asked, seem only to care
about Morocco, and to offer no more than Spain.)

When it comes to trade, Spanish answers are even less clear.
For example, in April 1987, Alfonso Guerra, vice-president of the
Socialist party, stated that "the EC should prepare generous
agreements providing for the absorption of manpower and the
enlargement of tariff preferences. Western Europe should plan
for the future integration of the Southern Mediterranean in its
economic system. . . ."[90] In Guerra's view, Tunisia and Egypt
should be key countries. But other government officials have told
this author that there is little that can be done for Mediterranean
countries in the area of trade, and that Spain will never allow the
Canary Islands to be treated less well than any of the
Mediterranean nonmember countries. Moreover, Spain will try
to include new agricultural products under the CAP regime and
prolong the periods of the year during which the principle of
Community preference is applied. Thinking has not gone
beyond these general statements.

As a country holding the EC Council of Ministers' presidency
in the first semester of 1989, Spain has given the Middle East top
priority in the Community's agenda. On the other hand it has not
shown particular interest for the Euro-Arab dialogue or the GMP.
Because of the contradiction between Spanish and Portuguese
agricultural interests and their strategic and financial stakes in
Mediterranean countries, the political line taken to date gives
priority to the political and financial component of EC relations
with the Middle East and Mediterranean. However, both Spain
and Portugal are prepared to make a special case of Morocco, in
response to a request from King Hassan II.

The Spanish Foreign Ministry has stated repeatedly that
Spain favors the "closest form of association" with Morocco that
is compatible with the Treaty of Rome.[91] Moreover, it is no secret
that Spain, like France, makes a sharp distinction between the
Eastern and the Western Mediterranean from a security
viewpoint; the former is seen as a disaster area to be kept as far
away as possible, as well as an area that falls under the
influence of the superpowers. On the other hand, in 1984, Spain
backed an unsuccessful initiative by French President Francois
Mitterrand to create a regional security system in the Western

Mediterranean. It also supported a similar Italian project, which Italian Prime Minister Bettino Craxi discussed with Prime Minister Gonzalez at a summit in Palma de Majorca, an initiative which Gonzalez took up with the governments of Tunisia and Egypt (which the Italians include in the system), early in 1987. Clearly, Spain would like to institutionalize summit meetings among Western Mediterranean countries, at either a bilateral or multilateral level.[92] This would be complemented by increased bilateral ODA to Morocco and Tunisia. In other words, Spain and Portugal could easily live with the long-standing U.S. position that the EC should have limited regional responsibilities. Neither of the new entrants has any particular interest in the EC Mediterranean Policy as it now stands, because it is essentially based on conceding special tariff preferences, and partly on EC imports that compete with imports originating in Spain and Portugal. According to various people consulted, vested domestic agricultural interests will dominate all others in this respect. Thus, Mr. Guerra's declarations notwithstanding, the Iberian countries will put a brake on any plan to further improve the EC's treatment of Mediterranean nonmembers. As one person interviewed put it, acrobatics will be the name of the game. Given the strategic, political and financial stakes involved, Spain's accession into the EC will certainly oblige it to look south. After all, NATO countries will be quite content with this division of labor, and the Spanish trade profile in the region is already quite high, as is shown by the enormous debts that Egypt ($1.5 billion) and Morocco ($400 million) owe Spain.

Some Thoughts on the Euro-Arab Dialogue

Because of the contradiction between Spain's agricultural interests, on the one hand, and its industrial, financial, and strategic ones, on the other, that country may be tempted to push for a renewal of the Euro-Arab dialogue inside the EC (as Greece tried in 1983) while trying to derail the EC Mediterranean Policy.[93] Some indication of this was given in the letter that Prime Minister Gonzalez sent to each Arab ambassador posted in Madrid at the time of the establishment of diplomatic relations between Spain and Israel in early 1986. In it, he states that Spain will try to contribute to the dialogue its knowledge and understanding of the sentiments of the Arab nations, underlining that the Enlargement will strengthen the contacts between the EC and the Arab world. [94] Until now, however, Spain has kept a very low profile with respect to the Euro-Arab dialogue, perhaps because of the complete failure of the Greek attempt, or because the price of oil is down from the 1983 level.

Among other things that Spain has done in this direction is to push, with Greece and Italy, to organize a meeting of the so-called troikas of the EC and the Arab League. (Portugal has not evinced any interest in the subject.) This is in line with Spain's belief that there must be an institutionalized dialogue to solve conflicts related to the Arab world, in order to reduce tensions in the Mediterranean and to fill the void created by the United States' loss of credibility in the Arab world. Moreover, Spain would not be averse to helping bring the Arab world closer to Latin America, again succumbing to the temptation to play the grandiose role of "bridge." But, it cannot bring up political conflicts of direct interest to itself (e.g., Ceuta and Melilla, and Algeria's protection of ETA terrorists) because neither the EC nor the Arab League would agree to tackle these subjects in the framework of the Euro-Arab dialogue.

Spain would like to address only political problems in the dialogue. However, because this is at variance with the position taken in the past by a majority of EC members it could pose problems to the Community itself, although these divergences will not come into the open as long as the Dialogue is not renewed. Nonetheless, the expectations of the Arab world have been raised because Spain may be able to influence the Euro-Arab dialogue in its favor.[95]

The Applications for EC Membership of Turkey and Morocco as New Issues for Spanish and Portuguese Diplomacy

The Turkish case. As with other EC members, neither Spain nor Portugal is in a hurry to state its position on this subject openly, letting Greece do the job of opposing Turkey's entry for them. For although Turkey is officially a secular state, both government circles and the press in Spain make it clear that most Turks believe in Islam. The weight of history should not be disregarded in this context altogether. (For instance, every Spanish child is taught in school that his country, representing Christianity, and the Ottoman empire, in the name of Islam, were at war in the 16th century.) The lack of respect for human rights by the present Turkish regime and the existence of a fairly important Islamic political movement in that country, are two elements that render

Spanish educated opinion apprehensive about considering Turkey a part of European civilization. Regarding other issues, however, Spain seems slightly less worried than Portugal, insisting that it has taken a neutral position with regard to the on-going Greek-Turkish conflict. "On the other hand, if this problem is solved, why not?" was the unofficial reaction to Turkish membership of someone close to the Spanish Foreign Ministry. And in another off-the-record remark, a Spanish official confessed that it would be particularly difficult for new members to say that "the boat is full" and there is no room for any more members. Portuguese officials queried mentioned competition in textile exports as a reason for acting with prudence in considering Turkey's application for EC membership. In addition, it is reasonable to expect both Portugal and Spain to be among those EC members who are reluctant to approve Turkish membership, simply because it would divert an important part of the structural funds in the EC budget away from Spain and Portugal. Neither Iberian country has political or strategic interests in this part of the Eastern Mediterranean. Thus, both Spain and Portugal will attempt to delay negotiations for Turkey's accession, but without calling too much attention to themselves.

The Moroccan case. The reaction to Morocco's application for membership in 1987 (that has since been turned down by the EC) is slightly different because, while both Portugal and Spain want Morocco to be anchored to Europe, the foreign ministries and national presses stressed that Morocco is not part of Europe and does not belong to either NATO or the Council of Europe. Some journalists called on their governments not to reject Morocco's request on mere geographical grounds,[96] as the Mediterranean was never a European frontier. However, the newspapers also made clear that stress should be laid on the democratic character of countries requesting to become EC members. After all, they pointed out, Spain and Portugal were not admitted into the EC until they met this condition set by the Community.[97] Thus, observers have viewed King Hassan's request for membership in the EC as a strategy: by asking the impossible, he hoped to get something substantial. In this, he seems to be counting on Spain and Portugal, among others, to support a closer association between Morocco and the Community—making Morocco a special case in the EC Mediterranean Policy. But, while the new entrants may push for Morocco's receiving the same "level of privilege" as Cyprus, Malta, and Turkey—which might imply, in the very long run, the creation of a Customs Union between the EC and Morocco and/or freedom of movement for workers between Morocco and the Twelve—anything more than this seems unlikely.[98] For example, Spain and Portugal would certainly object to Morocco's agriculture being covered by the CAP.

ACP Countries

The ACP Countries in Spanish and Portuguese Foreign Policy

Spain does not place sub-Saharan Africa among its top priorities for either economic or political diplomacy—except for Equatorial Guinea, a former colony. As explained above, its ODA for Africa will continue to be focused on this country, and on Portuguese-speaking countries. The latter can be taken as a gesture to Portugal, which will probably be quite happy to share the aid burden in this zone of the world with others. With regard to South Africa, because Spain has neither large economic interests nor a sizeable number of Spanish residents there, it will have a large margin of maneuver in handling the touchy issue of relations with Black and non-Black Africa. The Caribbean and Pacific countries come even further down on Spain's list of priorities than Africa.

Portugal has been a presence in Southern Africa for over five hundred years, its long history as a colonial power coming to an end with decolonization in 1974–1975. However, as Portugal had been developing intense economic relationships with EFTA countries since the 1960s, and especially because it has also had relations with the EC since 1972, decolonization came as less of a shock than might have been expected. Portuguese leaders seem to have transformed their philosophy within a very short period, all of them seeming to agree that, with the end of its colonial period, Portugal would have to rely on the help of European countries.

The Treaty of Accession to the Community should therefore be viewed as a simple development instrument. Not only was interest in Southern Africa lost very quickly in the years following Portugal's 1974 Revolution, but there were wars taking place in Africa as a consequence of the very rapid decolonization process. This lack of interest can also be explained by the sharp decrease in the share of Portuguese exports that went to Southern

Africa in the years preceding the Revolution: from around 25% in the years before 1970, to an insignificant percentage, and then back to only 5%.

The African country absorbing most of Portugals' exports was and still is Angola, a country the Portuguese consider extremely rich in natural resources. This, together with the fact that most of the 600,000 refugees arriving in Portugal after 1974 came from Angola, led Portugal to the conclusion that Angola could take care of itself, and that Portugal would do better to tackle development problems in cooperation with Europe. In other words, integration with the EC was taken as the new challenge after the end of the Empire. However, in the early 1980s, after a cooling-off period, Portugal again evinced interest in maintaining links with its old colonies, as France and the UK did with theirs in the 1960s. But, even today, relations are still fluid, because Portugal considers the ex-colonies a "hot potato," which should be treated with caution so that it does not become involved in their domestic politics.

On the other hand, Portugal has a rather high stake in South Africa because more than 600,000 Portuguese reside there. (Its other interests in that troubled country will be discussed when Portugal's position on EC matters regarding apartheid and sanctions are analyzed below.)

Spanish and Portuguese Views of their Roles in EC-ACP Relations

Spain has not hidden its limited interest in the ACP group of countries, despite the fact that this contrasts sharply with the situation in most other EC members. Thus, to the dismay of those attending the 1984 negotiations for renewal of the Lomé II Convention, where it had observer status, Spain made it clear that EC-Latin American links were among its top priorities in the EC, whether within or outside the context of the Lomé Convention. More recently, Luis Yañez, the state secretary for international cooperation and Iberoamerica, stated with some candor that Spain had very little to do with 50 out of 66 ACP countries and explained how he was surprised by the fact that when there is a discussion of developmental cooperation in the EC, it refers almost exclusively to Sub-Saharan Africa, while Central America is totally ignored.[99]

The attitude of Portugal is different. The Portuguese feel they know Southern Africa quite well because they were physically present there until 1974. On the other hand, prudence is the rule. Portugal does not see itself as a spokesman for its former colonies; the latter have not asked for this and could resent it. According to foreign ministry sources, Portugal's role in Angola and Mozambique should be limited to the economic and social domains, where Portugal's expertise (e.g., with tropical diseases) will continue to be appreciated. The possession of the appropriate technology for African countries is also mentioned as an asset by these officials. Moreover, its economic size, reduced foreign service, and the priority of domestic development, render the idea of being "Europe's door to Africa" one that has never been taken very seriously by most Portuguese politicians—in contrast with Spain's notion of its role in EC relations with Latin America. Portugal's modesty in this respect may also explain why it turned down the presidency of the EC Council of Ministers in the second semester of 1986, although it was Portugal's turn to hold that office.

Spain and Portugal's Past and Future
Contributions in Developing EC-ACP Relations

Since its accession to the EC, Spain seems to have changed its attitude toward the Lomé Convention slightly, in line with the principle: If you can't beat them, join them. As some Spanish experts put it, Spain has been obliged to contribute what amounts to 6.66% of the 6th EDF as from May 1, 1986 (about ECU 500 million) as part of adopting the acquis communautaire. Because this makes Spain the fifth largest donor in the Community, and because EC aid is "tied," Spanish enterprises should do everything possible to obtain contracts financed by the Community so that the ODA it channels through the EC is not wasted.

With regard to building up its image in Africa, since 1988, the Spanish Socialist government has been stressing that helping Angola and Mozambique is part of its anti-apartheid policies. This is in line with Angola's tremendously increased trade with Spain in recent years, Spain having become that country's second largest client (after the United States) and its fifth largest supplier.[100] Moreover, Spain has always stressed that both Angola and Mozambique are close to Spain culturally speaking and that the future looks bright for both countries—given Angola's economic potential and the existing trend toward democracy and ending its civil war. However, apart from this new focus, Spain will take a low profile in Africa because it has lost faith in its ability to obtain something similar to the Lomé Convention for Latin America.

From the Portuguese point of view, aid given through the Lomé Convention should be bolstered, because the Community has means that Portugal lacks to initiate a serious development policy in its former colonies—Angola, Mozambique, Sao Tome and Principe, the Cape Verde Islands, and Guinea-Bissau—all of which are members of Lomé Convention III. Indeed, even if this involves more outlays for the Portuguese Exchequer, Portugal will do its best and, it can be safely predicted, together with France, Britain, and Italy will be among the most sensitive countries with regard to aid requests from the sixty-six ACP countries.[101] Portugal will, however, be reluctant to support more EC trade concessions to ACP countries for fear of hurting its own economy.

The most potentially embarrassing demands made on Portugal by African countries have to do with South Africa, because Portugal would be "forced" to answer them in a negative way. For example, Portugal has, recently adopted a clear political line against excessive pressure or sanctions on South Africa, similar to the stances of the United Kingdom and the Federal Republic of Germany. This means that they do not consider sanctions useful and feel that instead of trying to isolate South Africa Western countries should try to maintain a dialogue with that country. To support this political line, Portugal has stressed that it understands both the region and the Afrikaaners well enough to know that any sanctions applied will backfire. Portuguese Foreign Ministry officials do, however, stress that their country is dead-set against apartheid and racism, which incidentally never existed in Portugal's former colonies. It should be noted that Portugal has been very actively engaged on this subject in the Community and takes a stand that is totally opposed to that of the four other Southern European EC members.

Behind the official explanation that sanctions are ineffective and counterproductive are additional reasons for Portugal's stand on the problem, that is, its lack of room to maneuver. One of them is Portugal's anxiety over the economic and social welfare of its 600,000 nationals residing in South Africa. Furthermore, many of the latter send part of their savings back to Portugal, bolstering the country's balance of payments. Portugal is also sensitive to possible cancellation of fishing rights granted by

South Africa off the coast of Namibia. Moreover, citizens of Mozambique now working in South Africa would suffer substantially from sanctions, because many of them would be dismissed if sanctions were applied. And, if South African Airways is obliged to stop using facilities on Cape Verde Islands as a result of EC sanctions, Cape Verde would lose the most important source of its foreign currency. In general, there is a large element of altruism in Portugal's favoring of former colonies, one that is particularly remarkable when Portugal's limited economic relations with South Africa are taken into account. According to foreign ministry sources, coal, which is Portugal's most important import from South Africa, can be obtained from other sources at any time. Moreover, Portugal does not benefit from the remittances of Portuguese workers there, because most Portuguese nationals residing in South Africa immigrated from Angola.

Thus, it would appear that Portugal's position on South Africa is not as heavily based on economics as that of the United Kingdom. Indeed, Portugal will always base its decisions on this matter more on what Angola and Mozambique have to say than on anything else.

To sum up, Portugal's views on the future of EC-ACP relations depend very much on which subject is brought up for discussion. There is no all-out support for the broadening of relations with ACP countries, as is apparent in the similar case of Spain and Latin America.

Links with the EFTA Countries

According to some official and unofficial declarations, Spain is interested in preserving and even developing EC relations with members of the European Free Trade Association, although this is not a priority area for either Spanish diplomacy or business. This is shown in Tables 2.1 and 2.2, which illustrate Spain's low trade profile with EFTA, especially since Portugal has withdrawn from that group. One exception may be Switzerland, due to the important investment flows between the two countries. The only item that has drawn Spain's attention to EFTA has been the early 1986 negotiations of the protocols for its adoption of EC-EFTA agreements, in which Spain tried to obtain highly advantageous terms from EFTA in compensation for what it perceived the unfavorable conditions it had to agree to in the

Treaty of Accession. However, the aim of obtaining immediate free access into EFTA countries for Spain's industrial exports was rejected outright by the latter. When the EC was unable to support Spain on this issue, it had to retreat.[102] According to some sources, however, Spain did manage to preserve what was most essential, that is, the degree of trade liberalization in agricultural products between it and EFTA countries that had been achieved in accordance with the 1979 agreement.[103]

Whereas the position of EFTA countries on trade in services is quite liberal, and they can be expected to strive to further deregulate EC-EFTA trade in this sector, Spain takes a somewhat protectionist stand on the subject. In view of all this, Spain will probably be among the EC members that are coolest toward new Community initiatives involving EFTA countries. This is already evident in the low-key irritation manifested in the Spanish press, [104] as well as in Spanish decisions regarding the initiatives of several EFTA countries to preempt further trade discrimination as an outcome of the completion of the EC's Internal Market in 1992.

Apparently, Spain fears overload if it is forced to eliminate all barriers to imports originating in Western Europe (and not only from the other eleven EC members) by the mid-1990s. Spain perceives the completion of the Internal Market as favoring countries with strong comparative advantages in the high-tech and service sectors, such as Britain or for that matter, EFTA countries. Why, the Spanish ask themselves, should EFTA countries benefit from the Internal Market, when a glance at the 1992 menu proposed by the Commission shows that agricultural exporters like Spain do not stand to gain very much? And, why should EFTA countries be able to chose those items in the process of European integration that suit them, without having to sacrifice anything, when both old and new full members of the club do not have the same option? Finally, why should Spain have to be subjected to Community discipline in order to reap membership benefits, when EFTA countries are not?

Spain's opposition to integration "a la carte" has led Spanish decisionmakers to the idea that European countries that want to benefit from the Internal Market should also have to contribute toward strengthening its cohesion by participating in "solidarity efforts." What this basically means is that EFTA countries should be required to contribute in one way or another to the EC's structural funds. It also means that EFTA countries should only benefit if they reciprocate by further opening their agricultural markets to EC products, in addition to making concessions in the industrial and service branches. It goes without saying that what Spain has in mind here are its own fruit, vegetable, flower, wine, and fish exports. Another possibility would be to obtain bilateral concessions—mainly from Switzerland—in the treatment of Spanish migration. Some Spanish observers even argue that opening a market of 320 million people to EFTA countries, against full access to economies more than ten times smaller, is not enough. They would require still another kind of reciprocity, although exactly what this would imply has not yet been specified.

Exports of Portuguese wine and textiles to Scandinavia (in particular to Sweden) are a significant component of total Portuguese exports. And, even though Portugal left EFTA in 1986, there is an important link still remaining: EFTA's Industrial Development Fund for Portugal, which was created in 1977. By providing $130 million in the last decade, the fund helped finance 435 projects representing a total investment of $340 million, the creation of 4,300 new jobs, and the preservation of 60,000 existing jobs.[105] As this continuing support is highly appreciated by the Portuguese, experts see Portugal as a future advocate for EFTA in the EC.[106] While entering the EC was necessary to make rapid economic development a reality, Portugal will not forget that its economic integration into Europe began with its successful membership in EFTA. How strong an advocate Portugal will be remains to be seen. Indeed, at least up to early 1989, Portugal adopted a very low profile on EFTA matters. However, it appears that Portugal will take a neutral stand, in regards to further developing EC-EFTA relations, one that is less cool than that of Spain but that is not too enthusiastic either. This is because its economic views on trade in services and in textiles do not coincide with those defended by EFTA countries in GATT.

EC Relations with Asian Countries

With the obvious exception of the Philippines—which Spain intends to include among future beneficiaries of its ODA— relations with the Asian continent have never been a priority for Spain. Indeed, Asia is called the "third step," after Latin America and the Mediterranean, in the Spanish Foreign Ministry, and it is not even clear whether Asia comes ahead of sub-Saharan Africa. While Spain would like to intensify relations with Japan and China because of their economic importance, there is no sensitivity whatsoever toward India, Southeast Asia, or Australia. On the other hand, although Asia is not a major priority in Portuguese foreign relations, there are still many reminders of the Portuguese colonial presence in Japan, China, India, and Thailand. For example, in April 1987, Portugal reached an agreement with China for the decolonization of Macao, which sits at the doorstep of that vast Asian country. Moreover, according to semi-official sources, Portugal would approve a formal broadening of EC relations with Asia, particularly with Japan.

EC-United States Relations[107]

In contrast with the scheme used for analyzing other geographical areas, this section will not focus on Spanish and Portuguese relations with the United States, because this would require the treatment of defense and strategic questions that lie outside the boundaries of this work. The discussion will therefore be restricted, as far as possible, to the economic aspect of EC-U.S. relations, as affected by the Iberian countries' entry into the Community. On the other hand, because both the United States and the EC are trading superpowers with worldwide economic interests the impact on EC-U.S. relations of changes in EC trade policies vis-a-vis different areas of the world or in GATT, as a result of the last Enlargement, will be assessed. One way to approach the subject is to ask how the Twelve compares with its rival trading partner, namely the United States. And, what emerges is that, in several domains, the Twelve tends to become much more similar to the United States than were the Ten in the ways discussed below.

The enlarged EC becomes an agricultural and fishing superpower represented in practically all important world food markets due to a significant increase in its fruit, vegetables, rice, olive oil, and wine profile. In mid-August 1987, the U.S. Department of Agriculture reported that the EC had replaced the United States as the world's leading exporter of agricultural products. That this is at least partly due to the EC Enlargement is evinced, for example, by the fact that in 1986 the Twelve exported $28.1 billion in farm products in comparison with the United States' $26.1 billion. The figures for 1976 were $11.8 billion and $23 billion, respectively. While other factors, such as exchange-rate changes and export subsidies, help to explain this spectacular increase, there is no doubt that the incorporation of Spain and Portugal into the EC has pushed the latter into the agricultural superpower club. In terms of fishing exports, Portugal and Spain's accession to the Community has increased EC exposure to the Atlantic Ocean by about 15%, which naturally has a significant effect here.

According to GATT and EC sources, the EC Twelve strengthens its salience in tourism activities, over the Ten, because the Iberian countries' revenues from international tourism is about 5% of their GDP, while the corresponding figure for the Ten is 1.5%.

Finally, the Community of Twelve strengthens its status as a first world trading power, which automatically increases its weight in GATT and the United Nations Conference on Trade and Development (UNCTAD).

There are two factors, in which the Enlargement increases the difference between the United States and the EC as trading blocs: (1) The EC-12 will have to be more sensitive than previously to the problems of the "South," and therefore relatively less interested in the problems of post-industrial societies; and (2) because the share of the Community's population with languages other than English as a mother tongue increases, the EC will be more sensitive to the dangers of cultural invasion. (However, in this connection, the United States is also becoming more of a multilingual society.)

In terms of the Community's present realm of activities, the two trading blocs look increasingly similar. For instance, the Enlargement will have a strong impact on EC-U.S. relations connected with CAP matters. The effects will be less marked in connection with EC Common Commercial Policy or Fisheries Policies. And, finally with respect to transatlantic monetary relations, there will be no change. But, if important questions in the realm of tourism, the mass media, or culture (e.g., in the domain of satellite communications) are included on the agenda of EC-U.S. relations, it can be assumed that the last Enlargement will make a difference.

Although the United States could not ignore the Community in GATT, even when it comprised only six members, the United States could ignore European Political Cooperation or Annual Summitry. However, the adoption of the Single European Act, together with the accession of Spain and Portugal, will change this to some extent. For example, although, the first official visit to Community headquarters by a U.S. president did not take place until 1978, we can expect such official contacts to become more frequent now. In the same vein, the voice of the president of the EC Commission should also weigh more when it is raised in the Annual Summit meetings of the seven largest industrialized Western Countries (as for instance in the July 1989 Paris Summit).

The next question to be considered is how Spanish and Portuguese inputs into the design of EC policies will affect the economy of the United States. In this connection, we begin by discussing the effect on various economic sectors, and then on the EC's system of external economic relations, specifying the geographical areas where the entry of Spain and Portugal might have an influence.

The Common Agricultural Policy (CAP)

The analysis presented until now leads to the conclusion that Spain will probably adopt a protectionist stance in agricultural matters in the short run, most likely by lining up with France to preserve the acquis communautaire,[108] but that this tendency will be somewhat counteracted by Portugal's more liberal position.

In the case of trade conflicts with the United States, however, both countries must take the global picture into account. That is, the Spanish government may shut its eyes to U.S. attempts to obtain an exceptional suspension of the principle of Community preference when this benefits Spanish consumers without hurting local agriculture. Indeed, this is what did happen when a trade war between the United States and the EC was on the verge of exploding on a subject of interest to the two new entrants. Thus, when U.S. corn exports to Spain were curtailed,[109] in line with the principle of Community preference, and the United States threatened to retaliate, the Commission had to retreat when its threats of counter-retaliation did not work. This was the first instance in which the principle of Community preference was abrogated. However—even though this could constitute a precedent—neither Spain nor Portugal were overexcited, most likely because both countries benefited in this particular case. This is because, until 1990, Spain is allowed to buy 2 million tons of corn from third countries and Portugal 300,000 tons of sorghum annually, *at reduced tariffs*. Moreover, the clause in the Accession Treaty obliging Portugal to reserve 15% of its cereal markets to EC suppliers was suspended at about the same time.[110]

From the above, we can conclude that, not being a founding member of CAP, Spain will not defend Community preference as a matter of principle; all will depend on the farm sectors being discussed. For instance, if the United States should question reference prices applied on EC citrus imports, Spain would be likely to invoke the principle as sacrosanct. Another indication of Spain's pragmatism on the issue was the case of a proposed tax on vegetable fats, which has left the Spanish government quite embarrassed. For, while the proceeds of such a tax would partly go to support the Community's olive oil producers, Spain fears that, if animal fats are not taxed, there will be a decrease in the relative consumption of olive oil, over and above the quantitative restrictions to be imposed on production. Unlike Portugal, the fear of reprisals by the United States do not play a central role for Spain.

Another touchy issue will be export restitutions (i.e., subsidies). As an important exporter of fruit, vegetables, wine, and olive oil, Spain will want to have its products covered by the CAP system, which has led the Community to dump goods such as wheat and dairy products on the world market at unrealistically low prices in recent years. The present degree of market organization for most Mediterranean fruit and vegetables does not allow for export restitutions to be applied except in very special cases; nor does it allow for guaranteed prices to farmers. On the other hand, olive oil, wine, and tobacco are covered by the system. However, it is well known that the United States has made it a priority in the Uruguay Round Negotiations to eliminate agricultural export subsidies. Thus, Spain, which has much to gain potentially from the present CAP system after the transition period, will oppose any Community moves acquiescing to U.S. desires. Portugal, on the other hand, will line up with EC countries that wish to minimize friction between the United States and the Community on export subsidies. This is because not a single of the few products it exports overseas competes with U.S. exports in third countries. This is clearly not true for Spain, for example, in the case of citrus fruit.

Uruguay Round Negotiations on
Industrial Products and Services

Spain and Portugal will be among the EC countries that are most reluctant to offer concessions in high-technology products or services, on the basis that their effort to open markets to EC and

EFTA countries in the coming years should be enough. In this regard, Portugal has already asked the Commission to be prudent in its plans for applying the resolutions adopted by GATT Contracting Parties on the rollback of protectionist measures.[111]

On the export side, both Spain and Portugal will request that the Commission includes additional products in the list of concessions presented to the United States (and to Japan). (Products generally included up to now have been chemicals and high-technology.) An occasion to submit such requests to the Commission will, of course, be when negotiating on tariff concessions in the context of the Uruguay Round of Multilateral Trade Negotiations scheduled to be completed by the end of 1990.

Common Policies in Respect to Fisheries

As emphasized by George Yannopoulos,[112] Spain and Portugal must be integrated into the EC fisheries treaty with the United States. At present, two bilateral fishery agreements allow the two new entrants to fish in the economic zone of the United States. As with Morocco, the United States will try to make approval of any new agreement between the EC and the United States conditional on concessions in other fields. Because fishing rights are very important to Spain and Portugal, the issue will then be which products the Community will include in its list of trade concessions. The real question here is whether other EC members are prepared to share the burden with Spain and Portugal, or whether they will stand on the principle the two Iberian countries should bear the full burden because it is they who will benefit from the new agreement.

The EC System of External Economic Relations

Spain does not question EC policies regarding the definition of geographical areas in which the Community wishes to have an impact. On the contrary, the question is not *if* or *how*, but *where*. On the other hand, the United States has long been a critic of the EC Mediterranean Policy for undermining the GATT system based on the unconditional most-favored-nation clause. As previously discussed, Spain would like the EC to consider special and exclusive tariff preferences for Central American countries in future agreements. Theoretically, then, this could aggravate the conflict between the United States and the EC, not only because it would extend a system already rejected by the United States to even more countries, but also because it would cover an area where the United States believes it has exclusive responsibility. Of course, Spain (and the EC) will counter by saying that the United States has revised its own long-standing doctrine on special preferences, for example, by launching its own "Caribbean Basin Initiative."

This leads to the real question of the Community's margin of maneuver in Central and South America. To be sure, the fact that Spain and Portugal are ex-colonial powers is reflected in their foreign policies, which—like those of the UK and France—are not geared solely towards Europe.[113] Their history, language, and location tended to make them interested in other areas of the globe: the Mediterranean and Latin America, for Spain; and Southern Africa, for Portugal. This analysis has shown Spain's intentions and aims regarding Central and South America, as well as toward the EC Mediterranean Policy and the Euro-Arab dialogue. It has also shown what the outcomes are likely to be.

The United States will never be enthusiastic about such increased influence by the EC. Here one should remember that, when Henry Kissinger was in charge of the U.S. foreign diplomacy, he assigned only limited regional responsibilities to the EC. Thus, reference must be made to the political as well as the economic component of EC policies, for instance, to the fact that Spain's desire to institutionalize the EC dialogue with all Central American Republics (including Nicaragua) does collide with U.S. views, and that Spain is highly critical of U.S. policies in Central and South America. One example of the latter is the strong criticism that Spain addressed to the United States when the United States invaded Grenada in October 1983. Less conflictive are the two countries' positions on Mediterranean and Arab-related affairs because Spain has now adopted a much less active profile on the subject and its position has slowly converged with that of the majority of EC countries. Moreover, in January 1986, Spain established diplomatic relations with Israel at the highest level, in contrast to Greece's stance in the EPC on the Middle East and Libya. This change in profile is in line with the rationale that Spain should only adopt controversial positions related to conflicts that do not endanger its own interests. On issues that hold no consequence for Spanish interests—as with South Africa—Spain might even dare to pull the EC in a direction opposite to the one adopted by the United States.

If the above analysis is correct, it appears that Spain will not try to address the security and political problems of the Mediterranean area in the EC unless Spanish interests are endangered. Thus, if Ceuta, Melilla, or the Canary Islands were at risk, Spain would try to mobilize the Community in the likelihood that NATO would refuse to deal with the matter.[114] Of course, in such an extreme case, U.S.-Community relations might be affected.

Thus, with respect to spheres of influence, the new Enlargement leads to some symmetry in the relations of the two trading superpowers with the South, where there was none previously. In addition to the traditional interest for Africa and the Arab world, there will now be a Latin American dimension as well. This will be perceived by the United States as leading to EC encroachment into a region where the United States has had a near-monopoly in the definition of international relations. However, because the Community starts at a very low level of relations with Latin America, any divergences with the United States will only constitute an element of irritation or annoyance for the American superpower. Nonetheless, it may lead the United States to consider the possibility of counteracting certain Community moves by offering some Latin American countries the kind of exclusive agreement achieved with Israel in September 1985 and with Canada in January 1988.

Convergence and Divergence of Spanish and Portuguese Views on the EC's External Economic Relations

This section evaluates the "net addition" implied by the two new entrants in terms of various EC policies in several areas of the world. If there is strong similarity of views between Spain and Portugal, the Iberian input should be noticed in Brussels. If, on the other hand, the views of Spain and Portugal neutralize each other, the net change in EC positions will be less substantial; here it must be emphasized that Spain carries more weight than Portugal in the Community's institutions and decisionmaking machinery.

The Portuguese have insisted on the need for their country to keep its national identity, which could be endangered by Enlargement. The fear here is that free trade in goods, capital, and manpower—together with the lack of important physical barriers between the two countries and the fact that the two national languages are similar enough for them to be learned easily by the neighbors—might blur the distinction between Portugal and Spain. And, the last thing that the Portuguese want is a "Benelux" in the Iberian Peninsula.

One way for Portugal to strengthen its national identity is to point out the differences in the two countries' foreign policies. Thus, Portuguese officials always stress that there will only be a convergence of views in some cases, for example in budgetary policies, the internal market, and cohesion, all of which concern domestic economic matters within the Community, where the two countries do coincide. However, where external relations are concerned, a distinction must be drawn between EPC and the rest. Because EPC deals with "high politics," it is not surprising that divergence seems to be the rule. Examples of sharp differences in this domain are EC relations with South Africa and, to some extent, with the United States. A distinction must also be drawn between general external economic policies and EC economic policies in different geographical areas. Here, there is more overlapping of positions with regard to the former than the latter. For instance, both countries follow similar lines on GATT negotiations and on the EC's Common Policies in respect to fisheries,[115] but there is open opposition and even rivalry in matters relating to Latin America. For example, Spanish officials cannot understand the Portuguese position of singling out Brazil from the rest of Latin America,[116] and this angers them because the area is so important to them.

Another interesting case is that of the GMP, where the record is mixed. For instance, both Spain and Portugal are in favor of strengthening Community relations with Morocco and in almost full concordance on Turkey's application for EC membership. But Portugal is not interested in other aspects of the Mediterranean Policy, while Spain is. However, this does not necessarily mean that the two positions effectively neutralize each other. On the contrary, for although Portugal is not affected very much by the renewal of the Mediterranean Policy, it did support Spain on the issues connected with it, albeit with little enthusiasm. What was probably behind this move was Portugal's thinking that it, too, might someday be in the position of exporting fruit and vegetables that compete with Mediterranean nonmembers. In this respect, the Portuguese will support Spanish attempts to increasingly organize wine, fruit, and vegetable markets in the context of the CAP, but it will always maintain a low profile in the matter.

On the other hand, Portugal is much more active than Spain in the Lomé Convention. However, Spain will not try to neutralize Portugal in this context.

Despite official declarations to the contrary, Portugal will adopt as low a profile as Spain with regard to relations with the EFTA. But here the interests of the two countries do not coincide product-wise; Portugal follows everything concerned with access to textile markets very closely, whereas Spain is interested in other industrial as well as agricultural products.

Portugal seems slightly more sensitive than Spain to matters having to do with EC policy toward Far Eastern countries, while the reverse holds true for relations with the Arab world. But neither of the two new entrants will be very active in developing EC external economic relations with these geographical areas.

On the other hand, the state of EC economic relations with the United States is crucial to both Spain and Portugal with regard to the supply of cereals and feed-grains. Thus, both countries will tend to vote together on matters relating to continental agricultural products. They will try to minimize trade diversion against the United States, although Spain will put less emphasis in this endeavor than Portugal, because it is an agricultural exporter itself and, as such, is very much aware of the importance of keeping the principle of Community preference intact.

When Spanish and Portuguese experts were consulted on whether Spain would have more influence in EC-decisionmaking than Portugal, there was a divergence of opinion, Spaniards naturally answered positively, whereas Portuguese answered negatively. According to the latter, all will depend on the subject being treated. This was also the reply given to the related question of whether Portugal would join other Southerners in the Community for voting purposes. While Italy, Spain, and Greece are expected to band together often, this will not apparently apply to Portugal.

To sum up, it would appear that the net effect of having the two Iberian countries add their vote in Brussels will vary depending upon subject and area. A ranking of the different policy items, according to the importance of their net effect (in descending order), is given below:

1. Domestic EC economic matters (e.g., budget, internal market)
2. Continental products in the CAP and economic relations with the United States

3. Mediterranean products in the CAP
4. EFTA
5. Morocco's application for membership in the Community
6. Mediterranean Policy.
7. Turkey's application for membership in the EC
8. The Lomé Convention.
9. EC relations with Latin America.
10. European Political Cooperation (e.g., in South Africa)

It must be stressed here that a large net effect does not necessarily imply that the impact of the Enlargement on EC decisionmaking is going to be stronger than if the net effect is small. It only means that if Spain and Portugal are both willing to act in the same direction, they will have a better chance of succeeding in influencing decisionmaking. This is true, for example, in connection with CAP policies on wine, where both countries have substantially the same interests and both want to change things in relation to the past. On the other hand, the large net effect in EFTA matters does not mean that the Iberian input will be noticed, because neither Spain nor Portugal has any substantial interest in the subject. It only means that the potential for impact is larger than, say, on EC policies in Latin America, where the strong views of the two new members seem to collide.

5

Summary and Conclusions

An enlargement of the European Community to include a fairly large country and a small one, such as the one that took place in 1986, cannot be considered a marginal change either by European or world standards. For, the accommodation of two newly industrializing countries with important but still unexploited agricultural potential into a free trade club of rich but aging industrial nations must have destabilizing effects in the short and medium run.

Free trade affects the domestic distribution of income in each member country as well as that among Community members. In the short run, factors of production linked to import-competing sectors must adjust, retreat, or face unemployment, while income received by factors working for export sectors tends to increase. In the medium run, the functional distribution of income tends to change too, favoring factors relatively abundant in each country to the detriment of those that are scarce. The more dissimilar the economic structures of the new member countries are in comparison with the old ones, the larger the changes will be. This is exactly the case in the third Enlargement of the European Community.

Not surprisingly, many experts expect the internal cohesion of the EC to be impaired if nothing drastic is done to prevent such a natural evolution. Aggravating this prognosis is the 1985 decision of the older member countries to eliminate all nontariff distortions affecting intra-Community trade in goods, services, and factors of production by January 1, 1993. Official aims of absorbing the two new members, and of completing the Internal Market without a strong basis of internal solidarity, may both backfire. One of the likely outcomes of such a backlash would be more Community protectionism against nonmembers, which would represent an indirect repercussion of the last Enlargement going far beyond the effects deriving from the mechanical application by Spain and Portugal of the acquis communautaire, as provided for in the Treaties of Accession of June 12, 1985.

When compared to the Community of the Ten, the Twelve is much larger geographically and demographically, as well as more diverse culturally. Its center of economic gravity shifts southward, and its agricultural, fishing, and touristic profile is enhanced. An increase in regional income disparities and a decrease in GDP per capita are also an inevitable outcome of the incorporation of the two Iberian fellows. For cultural, historical, economic, and demographic reasons, the new Community is also one that has more affinities with specific areas of the world. For example, Latin America, Southern Africa, the Middle East, and the Maghreb occupy a much less peripheral place in Spanish and Portuguese foreign policies than in those of most other EC members. On the other hand, relations with OECD nonmembers of the Community (e.g., Scandinavia and Japan) tend to take a backseat, occasionally even bordering on animosity (e.g., Spanish views on U.S. policies regarding NATO, Central America, and the Middle East).

To sum up, the power and influence of the Community in the world after the Enlargement is enhanced only in a few domains—whenever the weight added by Spain and Portugal compensates for the increasing lack of internal cohesion in the Community. Examples of this are international negotiations dealing with agriculture or relations with Latin America and the Gulf countries. On the other hand, tensions derived from disparities within the Community, and the fight for achieving internal compensations, will inhibit the Community's room for maneuvering in relations with third countries and will thereby increase the temptation to shift domestic instability outside.

The new members will also try to fight "reverse trade diversion," whenever and wherever this crops up as a result of Enlargement. For instance, they will try to prevent tourists from choosing less expensive destinations by trying to take group action at the Community level to counteract this trend. On the other hand, they will also try to minimize trade diversion in temperate-zone products, mainly because this would hurt their own consumers. And, if this also has the side effect of improving EC-U.S. relations, all the better.

Contrary to broad opinion, however, the Community's trade relations with third countries will not be enhanced by the last Enlargement. This is so because, in the short run the two new members will be reluctant to open their markets much beyond

what their Treaties of Accession compel them to do. They will also try to minimize domestic and external trade creation in the Community itself (e.g., regarding the internal market or GATT negotiations) insofar as trade in services and in industrial products are concerned. In order to prevent their countries and the EC from having too poor an image overseas, they will continually propose that the Community grant more aid, instead of still more trade concessions. These tactics will be defended in the context of discussions on the Lomé Convention and the Mediterranean Policy. But Spain and Portugal's positions will not carry much weight because their credibility is low (due to their ODA as a percentage of GNP falling very far below the OECD average of 0.36%).

Another reason for trade relations with third countries not being enhanced is the Portuguese government's stress on the economic development of their own country and Spain's wanting its Mediterranean agriculture to reap all possible benefits from CAP and EC structural funds. Moreover, the Community at Twelve "feels" poorer than ever, and is currently concentrating on important domestic projects such as the successful completion of the Internal Market by 1992.

In the past, observers of the Community's external economic policies have been struck by the existence of a quite rigid (though unofficial) hierarchy of privileges granted by the Community to different countries of the United Nations.[117] At the very top are, of course, members, followed by countries in EFTA, and then the Lomé Convention. Before the Southern Enlargement, the three Mediterranean countries applying for membership were usually placed after Lomé Convention countries and before Mediterranean Policy countries, and Turkey, Malta, and Cyprus (the latter three of which are potential members of the EC and have association agreements with the EC). Next come all other developing countries (including China) that are only benefiting from the Community's GSP scheme. Last on the list—but not least—are nonpreferred countries, including the United States.

After the Southern Enlargement, Greece, Spain, and Portugal are, of course, in the First League, a promotion that may explain Spain's new paternalistic attitude toward its Mediterranean neighbors, who are considered to belong to another world because they do not happen to be members of the EC. This tendency is compounded by the fact that Spaniards think that because two of their nationals sit on the EC Commission their weight and clout in the Twelve is the same as that of other large Community members. Although this feeling of superiority is clearly illusory, it may be enough to allow them to continue in this direction.

It is important to realize that Spain and Portugal's higher places in the pyramid of privilege will dominate any other alteration in the hierarchy of agreements and policies in the EC system of foreign economic relations. For, not only will the new members rank higher in the pyramid themselves, but now that they belong to the group of countries able to influence the position of nonmembers in the pyramid of influence, or the hidden face of the pyramid of privilege, they can naturally be expected to defend their interests in the Community. They cannot be expected to defend the policies of other Community members or of third countries, except in marginal cases where the stakes involved for the new entrants are negligible. For instance, both Spain and Portugal will try to maximize trade diversion in wine, fruit, and vegetables by proposing modifications in the CAP, but not necessarily in the highly visible Mediterranean Policy. Both will strongly defend the principle of Community preference in agriculture, which can only mean more protectionism against the other Mediterranean producers of fruit, vegetables, and olive oil. All this implies a further raising of fences between the Community and the Mediterranean Basin, a very dangerous strategy for the Community because of its energy dependence on the area as well as the importance of the basin's market for European goods and services.

To extract itself from this dilemma, the Community might be tempted to shift the burden even further onto other Third World countries, thereby trying to maintain some semblance of preference for Mediterranean countries. But this strategy is not likely, because the new members are far from wanting any further discrimination against Africa and Latin America, though there are some possibilities in this direction with regard to Asia. It is much more likely that the EC will raise the political and financial components in its relations with Mediterranean countries to compensate for increasing restrictions on trade and labor movements.

If this happens, the new entrants may have a larger influence on the Mediterranean Policy of the Community than (as is commonly assumed) on EC-Latin American relations. This is because their basic strategy is to erode, detract, or derail what has already been achieved, not to add to it. And, because the Luxembourg compromise—conferring virtual veto power on any and all EC members in important decisions—is still alive and well, the possibilities of action are disproportionate. For, it is easier to deny or block policies than to initiate and win approval for new ones, because the latter requires several allies (which Spain will have difficulty in finding as far as Latin America is concerned, because of the general reluctance to confront the United States). Moreover, as Spain and Portugal generally agree on what should or should not be done with respect to Mediterranean nonmembers (e.g., strengthening Morocco's ties to the Community, postponing Turkey's entry *ad infinitum*, and giving the Canary Islands' agriculture an edge over that of Southern Mediterranean countries), their individual possibilities of influencing EC policymaking are strengthened.

The fact that Morocco will become one of the rare candidates for promotion in the hierarchy of EC trade agreements is both remarkable and important. This could not have occurred before Spain and Portugal entered the Community. Under pressure from the two new member states, Morocco will be singled out for special, more favorable, treatment compared with the other Mediterranean Policy countries.

Other countries in the Third World, especially the Arab countries and countries of Central America, will be disappointed when they will realize that the enlarged Community will be offering them political declarations rather than new trade concessions, or increased financial aid.

This should not come as a surprise because the slight changes in the Community's external trade dependence levels (increasing slightly in relation to Latin America and the Middle East, and decreasing somewhat in relation to EFTA) do not justify any more action or any change in the order of the Community priorities that dominate its trade policies.

This is even more true with regard to EC relations with developing countries, because Spain and Portugal are now totally integrated into the developed world, as is evinced by the intense financial and human exchange between them and the rest of the Community, the United States, and Switzerland. Spain's sensitivity vis-a-vis Latin America derives from an above average interdependence in terms of finance and migration, but not in terms of trade. Although Spain might like it to be otherwise, it is trade and not (yet) investment or migration policy that is conducted at the Community level. And this is precisely why it seems difficult to envisage the creation of a new category—Latin America policy—in the EC system of external trade agreements. For, the first question that arises is where such a policy would rank in the ladder of privilege, and—in view of the analysis made earlier—it is clear that Spain's ambition of placing it at the level of the Lomé Convention and beyond the class of the Mediterranean nonmembers seems unwarranted. (It is significant that Spain's ambition of bolstering EC-Latin American links will be hampered, to some extent, by Portugal's obstructive attitude.) From a strict realpolitik viewpoint, a Latin America policy should fall between the Mediterranean Policy and the EC's GSP. Also, in connection with the Southern Cone countries—which are the ones that everybody in the EC cares about for economic reasons—a Lomé-type solution would be wrong, because they are NICs, in the same category as Israel, Turkey, Malta, Cyprus, and even Egypt. It is for this reason that a solution for Argentina, Brazil, Uruguay, and Chile, along the same lines of partial reciprocity being applied to Israel and Turkey, does not seem implausible. Such a solution would tend to reduce the area's trade dependence on the United States. Although this is a major aim of many Latin American politicians, it is quite another matter to convince them that two-way free trade will benefit them as well, especially because all Mediterranean non-EC members, with the exception of Israel, do not seem to have been convinced by this argument, and even in Israel many still see tariff dismantling as the price they must pay for free access into Community markets! Based on this analysis, it is obvious that the new entrants will have more chance of affecting EC Mediterranean Policy than EC-Latin American relations.

Another difficulty in implementing a Latin American policy is that, for obvious reasons, the United States will probably be against whatever the EC proposes to Latin American countries. Although the arguments used in GATT and other forums depend on what the Community actually proposes, it seems clear that the United States will have more difficulty now than in the early seventies in pointing an accusing finger at EC bilateral trade strategies at variance with the multilateral, nondiscriminatory approach of GATT. For it too has set up bilateral trade agreements with Israel and Canada, and has understandings (e.g., with Japan) that are ironically called "voluntary" export restraints.

With regard to foreign economic relations, neither a Southern nor a Mediterranean lobby will form in the Community. This contrasts with EPC or domestic EC matters such as budgetary policies, support for Mediterranean agriculture, regional policies, and, to some extent, questions related to the completion of the Internal Market. This is because the individual positions of the five Southern European Community members diverge substantially with regard to Africa, Latin America, the Middle East, and the United States— the main areas in which they might have some influence on EC decisionmaking.

Notes

Chapter 1

1. To illustrate Spanish pro-Europe enthusiasm, suffice it to say that according to polls made in the spring of 1989 81% of those asked were in favor of a referendum in each EC member country to establish a European Union, 78% were in favor of a European passport, and 67% were in favor of a European currency. *El País*, July 10, 1989.

2. See, e.g., the enormous work on this subject by Donges, J. et al. (1982), *The Second Enlargement of the European Community*, Tübingen, Mohr; Lorca, A. et al. (1984), *Un punto de vista español del área mediterránea como zona de interés prioritario*, Instituto de Economía Aplicada, September; Musto, S. (1983), "The European Community in Search of a New Mediterranean Policy: A Chance for a More Symmetrical Interdependence?" in Pinkele, C., and Pollis, A. (eds.), *The Contemporary Mediterranean World*, New York, Praeger, pp. 151–174; Pomfret, R. (1986), *Mediterranean Policy of the European Community*, London, Macmillan (for the Trade Policy Research Centre); Tovias, A. (1979), *EEC Enlargement: The Southern Neighbours*, Brighton, Sussex European Papers No. 5; Yannopoulos, G. (1988), *Customs Unions and Trade Conflicts*, London, Routledge.

3. See, Brugmans, H. et al. (1973), *The External Economic Policy of the Enlarged Community*, Bruges, De Tempel.

4. See, e.g., Yannopoulos, G. (1988), p. 25.

5. See, Tovias, A. (1977), p. 29.

6. Council of the European Communities (1985), *Instruments Concerning the Accession of the Kingdom of Spain and the Portuguese Republic to the European Communities*, Vols. I–III.

7. This scheme is adapted from Tovias, A. (1984), "The Effects of the Second Enlargement of the European Community upon Israel's Economy" in Gutmann, E. (ed.), *Israel and the Second Enlargement of the European Community: Political and Economic Aspects*, Jerusalem, The Hebrew University.

8. See, endnote 2.

9. See, e.g., Praet (1988)

Chapter 2

10. Our calculations in this section are based on World Bank and Eurostat data.

11. Including France, which generally considers itself a Latin country and which is in fact, Southern in terms of agriculture and tourism.

12. After the last EC Enlargement all the European members of the Atlantic Alliance except Norway belong to the Community.

13. Yugoslavia did conclude a Cooperation Agreement with the EC on May 22, 1980, providing among others for the duty-free import from Yugoslavia of industrial goods (except for textiles). The EC also eliminated quantitative restrictions on this Balkan country's imports. Later on, in mid-1981, a specific agreement on trade in textiles was signed, whereby Yugoslavia agreed for each Agreement year to restrain its exports to the EC of a list of products listed in an Annex.

14. Tovias, A. (1984), "The Effects of the Second Enlargement of the European Community upon Israel's Economy" in Gutman, E. (ed.), *Israel and the Second Enlargement of the European Community: Political and Economic Aspects*, Jerusalem, The Hebrew University, pp. 101–102.

15. See, *El País*, July 15, 1987.

16. See, Tovias, *ibid.*, p. 102.

17. See, Commission of the European Communities (1986), *The Tourism Industry and the Tourism Policies of the Twelve Member States of the Community*, Doc. VII/473/86–EN.

18. The right kept a majority of 222 facing a left of 215. The Christian Democrats are regrouped under the name of "European People's Party," while the Conservatives have chosen the name of "European Democrats." See *The Guardian*, November 3, 1986.

Chapter 3

19. Closely related to these figures are, of course, the shares of the five Mediterranean EC members in the population (53.2% in 1986) and in the GNP of the Twelve (45.9% in 1986). Note also that only a two-thirds majority in the Parliament is required to dismiss the Commission, to make decisions on the budget, or wherever the Parliament itself determines that such a qualified majority is warranted.

20. It is worthwhile, however, to note that there are exceptions to this rule, as when almost all the Spanish delegates voted for a Spaniard (Enrique Barón) to become president of the European Parliament in June 1989.

21. See *El País*, June 3, 1988, which pointed out that Spain would like to establish itself on the level of Great Britain and West Germany and would devote as many resources as those countries do to the presidency of the Council. Moreover, Spain also wanted at an early date to organize a special European Summit to explore the possibility of conferring more power on the European Parliament, a "grand design," which of course did

not materialize by 1989. Nor have Spain's grandiose plans for the reduction of the Latin American debt, suggested by the Prime Minister as late as the early months of 1989. See *El País Internacional*, February 6, 1989.

22. In this respect, Portuguese officials told this author that two assets would enhance Portugal's influence: (1) the tradition of cooperation with other Western countries (e.g., in NATO or in EFTA) and with former African colonies since their independence; and (2) Portugal's capacity to understand the policies of other countries.

23. Source: Boletín ICE, No. 2084, May 11–17, 1987; *Boletín Informativo Banco Central*, No. 440, June 1988; *Boletín Informativo Banco Central*, No. 452, June 1989. All percentages are calculated on the basis of figures in nominal terms (pesetas).

24. Ministerio dos Negocios Estrangeiros (1986), *Portugal Nas Comunidades Europeias, Primeiro Ano*.

25. Only about 20% of CAP-related expenditure is directed to supporting Mediterranean agricultural products. In this respect, see the very pessimistic assessment by Pomfret, R. (1986), *op. cit.*, p. 98.

26. Yannopoulos, G. (1987), "The Challenge of the Southern Enlargement of the European Community," *Il Politico*, No. 3, p. 435.

27. See Resoluciones, Congreso del PSOE, Madrid, December 13–16, 1984.

28. Grupo Socialista del Parlamento Europeo (1987), *España Europa: Trabajo Común, Los socialistas en el Parlamento Europeo*, p. 14.

29. Information and data obtained from the "Instituto para a Cooperacao Economica," Lisbon, Portugal.

30. Salgado Albor, J. (1987), "España en el Mundo Actual," *Boletín de Información*, No. 199, VII, CESEDEN, March.

31. See, for example, the current program of the Spanish Socialist Party: PSOE, *Programa 1986/1990*.

32. See, *Política Exterior*, Vol. I, No. 1, Winter 1987.

33. See, *El Periódico*, January 1, 1986.

34. Yannopoulos, G. (1987), p. 433.

35. A situation reminiscent of the mid-60s, when the standard answer of the Six to third countries' demand for association was that the EEC was too busy implementing the CAP and the Customs Union.

36. See, *The Economist*, "Two Sides of Europe," June 27, 1987. See also, Praet P. (1988), "The Change of the Baricenter of the EEC from a New Hanseatic League to a Southern-Oriented Community: A View from the Center," in *Jerusalem Journal of International Relations*, Vol. 10, No. 3, September, pp. 33–54.

37. See, *El País Internacional*, March 30, 1987.

38. Speech presented to the Congress of Socialist Parties in the EEC, Cascais, Portugal, May 5, 1987. The fact that the Southern countries' thesis has been adopted as the Commission's official line proves the political clout of Mediterranean countries among the Twelve.

39. *The Times*, November 20, 1987; Baron, E. (1989), p. 120.

40. See, e.g., *El País Internacional*, May 18, 1987, which devotes an article to the alleged lack of coordination between different Spanish ministries, as well as between Spain's permanent delegation in Brussels and the secretariat of state for the EC.

Chapter 4

41. The share of South America was even higher in the past. It dropped from a high of 53.34% in 1975–1979, to 42.16% in 1980–1984, to 22.6% in 1985.

42. A shorter version of this section was published by the author as an article under the title: "Iberian Countries, Iberoamerica and the European Community," *The World Economy*, Vol. 12, No. 1, March 1989, pp. 105–115.

43. See, for example, the declaration that Spanish Foreign Minister Fernandez Ordoñez made to *Política Exterior* in 1987; Vol. I, No. 1, Winter 1987, pp. 14–15.

44. Free translation by the author. Emphasis added.

45. *Boletín ICE*, Las inversiones directas españolas en el exterior durante 1985; No. 2026, March 10–16, 1986, pp. 851–858. Respective figures for investment in Europe were 32.65% and 37.76%.

46. See Tables 2.1 and 2.2.

47. Armero, J.J. (1989), p. 121.

48. See, Durán, E. (1985), *European Interests in Latin America*, Chatham House Papers, No. 28, p. 102.

49. As stressed by Sebastian, L. de, "¿España, es realmente puente entre Europa y América Latina?," *Muga*, September 1985, pp. 54–67.

50. "Elemento dinamizador." Sometimes the word "translator" is used by Spain in an attempt to show restraint and modesty. See Grugel, J. (1987), p. 605.

51. See, interview of Fernando Morán, former Spanish Minister in *Politique Internationale*, Paris, Winter 1983–84.

52. *El País*, March 24, 1988.

53. Grugel, J. (197), p. 605.

54. See, *El País Internacional*, January 12, 1987.

55. COM (1986) 720 December 2; and COM (1986) 6033, December 3.

56. Secretaría de Estado para las Comunidades Europeas (1987), pp. 63–64.

57. See also, Flores, E. (1987), Europa y América Latina, el desafío de la cooperación, *Leviatán*, No. 27, Spring, pp. 93–101. For an excellent survey of EPC issues of the Enlargement, see, Regelsberger, E. (1985), From Ten to Twelve: A New Dimension for the EPC, *International Spectator*, July–December, No. 3/4, pp. 34–44.

58. Council Regulation (EEC) No. 2009/86, June 24, 1986, *Official Journal of the European Communities*, L 172, Vol. 29.

59. See, Estrella, R. (1987), Europa y América Latina: La Cooperación al Desarollo, *Leviatán*, No. 27, Spring, pp. 103–112. In it, Estrella explains his frustration after several months working as a Eurodeputy at the European Parliament in making Spain's position understood or accepted by his non-Spanish colleagues. This frustration was compounded by the fact that not one of the foreign ministers of the largest four Community members was present at the third San José meeting (in Guatemala City), in February 1987. See also Piñol (1989), p. 19, which relates to the rejection by the EC of requests by Central American countries for more benefits under the EC's GSP at the "San José IV" conference in Hamburg in early 1988.

60. See, Tovias, A. (1987), "The Impact of the Second Enlargement of

the European Community on Latin American Economies," in Coffey, P. and Wionczeck, M. (eds.), *The EEC and Mexico*, Dordrecht, Martinus Nijhoff, p. 183.

61. On graduation, differentiation and conditionality in the application of GSP benefits, see, Weston, A. et al. (1980), *The EEC's Generalized System of Preferences*, London, Overseas Development Institute, pp. 165–176. Interestingly, Venezuela, Argentina, Uruguay, Brazil, and Mexico are all mentioned as possible candidates (others might say victims) linked to these innovations.

62. Grugel, J. (1987). p. 608.

63. See also, Rummel, R., Concentric Integration? The Impact of Greek, Spanish and Portuguese Membership on Western Europe as a Foreign Policy Actor, paper presented at the Sixth International Conference of Europeanists, Washington, D.C., November 1987.

64. See, Tovias, A., in Coffey, P., and Wionczeck, M. (1987), *op. cit.*, p. 182.

65. This can also be applied in the comparison between Spanish interests at stake in South and Central America.

66. See, e.g., Fernandez-Ordoñez, F. (1987), "Política Exterior de España 1987–1990," *Política Exterior*, Vol. 1, No. 1, Winter, p. 15.

67. Fuentes, J. (1986), "España y la Seguridad Internacional," *Revista de Estudios Internacionales*, Vol. 7, No. 4, October–December, pp. 1089–1105.

68. This perception ignores the incursion of Napoleonic troops into Spain, as well as other wars with France.

69. Libya officially defined Melilla as a Moroccan city under Spanish occupation in November 1985. See Armero, J.M. (1989), p. 205.

70. See, Schumacher, E. (1987), "Estados Unidos y Libia," *Política Exterior*, Vol. 1, No. 2, Spring, pp. 167–191. Algeria feared that Spain will allow NATO bases to be set in the Canary Islands in the future.

71. See, Descallar, J., *Cuestiones de interés permanente para España en el área mediterránea*, Madrid, Centro Superior de Estudios de la Defensa Nacional, no date.

72. Libya was the first crude oil and gas supplier of Spain in 1986.

73. In fact, Morocco, Algeria, Egypt, and Tunisia represented more than 63% of Spanish exports to the Mediterranean area in 1987.

74. At the same time, Egypt owed Spain about $1500 million.

75. Morocco is central for strategic reasons. See Lopez García, B. (1987), Marruecos y el Maghreb en la politica española, *Razón y Fe*, No. 1065, July–August, pp. 709–723.

76. In the case of Morocco, a controversy has erupted around the use of these funds; according to press reports, some of them were to finance arms exports.

77. See, *El País*, July 4, 1988.

78. This was confirmed in conversations with Socialist party officials.

79. *Boletín ICE*, No. 2051, September 22–28, 1986, pp. 3057–3060.

80. See, *El País*, April 5, 1987.

81. See, *El País*, October 22, 1986.

82. The concessions in question concerned twenty-three products, that is, seven more than those included in the 1970 EC-Spain agreement. See, Confederación Española de Organizaciones Empresariales (1987), *Primer Año. Balance de la Integración de España*, Madrid.

83. Negotiations with Morocco lasted until mid-1988, because it linked issues like fishing rights and the free passage of Moroccan trucks through Spain with the negotiations.

84. See, Ministerio dos Negocios Estrangeiros, *Portugal* (1986), *op.cit.*, p. 41.

85. In the opinion of this author, it is precisely the perspective of having to suffer from limitations imposed on agricultural exports that tipped the balance in Turkey in favor of those proposing an early application for membership into the EC, which was actually presented in the spring of 1987.

86. See, *Telex Mediterranée*, January 27, 1987.

87. See, *El País*, July 8, 1987, where it was announced that the Farmer's Union of Valencia would fight any change in the present *status quo*. See also, *El Independiente*, April 2, 1988.

88. *El País*, November 27, 1988.

89. Ioakimidis, P. C., "Community Financial Flows to Mediterranean Countries," paper presented at a Symposium on "Challenges to Mediterranean Cooperation and Security in the late 80's." Spetsae Island, Greece, May 28–31, 1987.

90. At the Council of the Socialist International in Rome.

91. See, e.g., *El País*, July 21, 1987.

92. This has even been proposed by Mr. Guerra to Algeria, which has been quite resistant in the past to this kind of idea. See, *El País Internacional*, December 29, 1986.

93. The Euro-Arab dialogue was launched in the wake of the Yom Kippur war in 1973 as requested by the Arab League, which wanted to discuss political issues, such as the Arab-Israeli conflict at the highest possible level between one regional bloc and the other. The dialogue was suspended by the Arab side after Egypt signed a Peace Treaty with Israel in 1979 and has not been officially renewed since then.

94. Armero, J. A. (1989), p. 217.

95. See, for example, *El País Internacional*, January 12, 1987. See also Al-Mani, S., and Al Shaikhly, S. (1983), *The Euro-Arab Dialogue*, London, Frances Pinter, pp. 88–89. In the eyes of the authors, the last Enlargement "would perhaps even change the Community's image abroad, from one of a Northern European power to that of a Mediterranean power. The political ramifications of such a change in image would perhaps involve the EC further in Mediterranean political problems."

96. See, *ABC*, July 25, 1987 and *El País*, July 29, 1987.

97. If this were one of the main requirements for entry, it would open the way for Israel's membership in the EC.

98. Apparently a request by Morocco for Portuguese diplomatic support to foster its candidacy was rejected.

99. *Le Courrier*, no. 103, May–June 1987, pp. 6–8.

100. See, the article of L. Yañez, Spanish State Secretary for International Cooperation and Iberoamerica, in *El País*, August 8, 1988.

101. For example, Portugal has pushed very strongly for increasing EC food aid to Mozambique. Its share in the present EDF is 0.88%.

102. As indicated in Chapter 1, the EC decided in early 1989 to advance to July 1 of the same year the date on which Spain's industrial exports shall get duty-free access to Community markets. Shortly afterwards, EFTA

countries, wanting to stay competitive with the EC, made the same offer to Spain.

103. This agreement also provided for the exchange of tariff preferences on industrial imports between Spain and EFTA.

104. See, *El País*, May 19, 1988

105. *Agence Europe*, November 6, 1986.

106. See also, Ministerio dos Negocios Estrangeiros, *Portugal, op. cit.*, p. 40.

107. The analysis presented here draws upon a paper submitted to a conference on U.S.-EC Relations at the University of Aix-en-Provence in October 1986. See Tovias, A., "L'impact du nouvel élargissement des Communautés Européennes sur les relations avec les Etats-Unis," in Bourrinet, J., (ed.) (1987), *Les relations Communaute Europeenne Etats-Unis*, Paris, Economica, pp. 159–168.

108. See, *International Herald Tribune*, August 11, 1986.

109. For an excellent survey of the conflict from an analytical viewpoint, see Yannopoulos, G. (1987), *The Trade Interests of the United States and the Enlargement of the EC*, University of Reading, Discussion Papers in European and International Social Science Research, No. 17, March.

110. Initially Spain did oppose the Commission's proposal out of fear that it would not be able to absorb the 2 million tons because they had recently changed the proportions of the various feeding grains used by Spanish farmers. To prevent the United States from punishing Spain for not keeping the agreement, Spain would have liked the EC to buy any unwanted quantities. See, *El País Internacional*, February 2, 1987.

111. Ministerio dos Negocios Estrangeiros, *Portugal, op. cit.*, p. 56.

112. Yannopoulos, G. (1987), *The Trade Interests, op. cit.*, p. 15.

113. See, *The Economist*, June 28, 1986, where the Spanish case is compared to the opposing ones of the Federal Republic of Germany and the Benelux countries.

114. There was a precedent when Libya announced raids on Italian and Spanish towns in retaliation for the U.S. raid on Tripoli. The Twelve answered by reducing the number of Libyan diplomats authorized to stay in the Community, and by tightening controls over visa deliveries. See, *ABC*, April 15, 1986.

115. The only point of possible conflict is a "domestic EC matter," namely, fishing rights for Spaniards in Portuguese waters.

116. There are even sharp divergences between the two Iberian countries on the issue of commemorating the fifth century of the discovery of America. Portugal does not want Spain to steal the show. Furthermore, it does not want to concentrate the celebrations in the year 1992, but to spread them throughout more than a decade, so as not to privilege the date of October 12, 1492.

Chapter 5

117. Sometimes called the "pyramid of privilege." See Weston, A. et al. (1980), *The EEC's, op.cit.*; Hine, R. (1985), *The Political Economy of European Trade*, Sussex, Wheatsheaf, pp. 95–99.

Bibliography

ABC, various numbers.

Agence Europe, various numbers.

Aldecoa, F. (1983), "Significado y efectos de la adhesión de España a la Alianza Atlántica en su proceso de participación activa en las relaciones internacionales," *Revista de Estudios Internacionales*, Vol.4, No. 1, January–March, pp. 39–70.

Aldecoa, F., and Najera, A. (1986), "España en las relaciones de la Comunidad Europea con América Latina," *Afers Internacionals*, No. 10, Winter, pp. 121–125.

Allen, D. et al. (1982), *European Political Cooperation*, London, Butterworths.

Allen, D., and Smith, M. (1983), "Europe, the United States and the Middle East: A Case Study in Comparative Policy Making," *Journal of Common Market Studies*, Vol. 22, No. 2, December, pp. 125–145.

Allen D., and Smith, M., "A New American Challenge? Reaganism, the 'New Cold War' and the Prospects for Foreign Policy Collaboration in Western Europe." Paper presented to UACES Annual Conference, January 1986.

Al-Mani, S., and Al Shaikhly, S., (eds.) (1983), *The Euro-Arab Dialogue*, London, Frances Pinter.

Anderson, K., and Tyers, R. (1986), "International Effects of Agricultural Policies," in Snape, R., *Issues in World Trade Policy*, London, Macmillan, pp. 93–114.

Anuario El País 1987.

Armero, J. M. (1989), *Política exterior de España en democracia*, Madrid, Espasa Calpe.

Ashoff, G. (1983), "The Textile Policy of the European Community towards the Mediterranean Countries: Effects and Future Options," *Journal of Common Market Studies*, Vol. XXII, No. 1, September, pp. 17–45.

Baklanoff, E. (1985), "Spain's Emergence as a Middle Industrial Power. The Basis and Structure of Spanish-Latin American Economic Interrelations," *AEI Occasional Papers*, No. 11, April.

Barbé, E. (1984), "La región mediterránea (I). El flanco sur de la OTAN," *Afers Internacionals*, No. 3, Spring, pp. 5–16.

Barbé, E. (1984), "La región mediterránea (II). La evolución de la estrategia americana," *Afers Internacionals*, No.4, Summer, pp. 5–16.

Barbé, E. (1984), *España y la OTAN*, Barcelona, Laia.

Barón, E. (1987), "España-Europa: Trabajo Común," *Leviatán*, No. 27, Spring, pp. 93–102.

Barón, E. (1989), *Europa 92, El Rapto del Futuro*, Barcelona, Plaza y Janes.

Berrocal, L. (1980), "El Diálogo Euro-Latinoamericano: Más allá de un Neocolonialismo larvado?," *Revista de Instituciones Europeas*, Vol. 7, No. 3, September–December, pp. 947–1067.

Berrocal, L. (1981), "La politique latino-americaine de l'Espagne. Quelques elements d'analyse," in Institut d'Etudes Europeenes, *La Communauté Européenne et l'Amérique Latine*, Brussels, Editions de l'Université de Bruxelles, pp. 187–218.

Berrocal, L. (1983), "L'Espagne et la coopération euro-arabe: Quel avenir dans une Europe élargie? Quelques hypothèses de travail," in Khader, B., *Cooperation Euro-Arabe*, Louvain, Université Catholique de Louvain.

Berrocal, L. (1986), *L'ouverture vers le Sud de la Communauté Européenne: Quelle perspective de développement?*, Brussels, Université Libre de Bruxelles, Doc. D.T. (86) 44.

Bodemer, K. (1985), "Perspectivas de las relaciones interregionales entre la Comunidad Europea y América Latina," *Integración Latino-americana*, April, pp. 22–31.

Boletín ICE, various numbers.

Bonvicini, G., "Achievements and Perspectives of EPC," Rome, Istituto d'Affari Internazionali, unpublished paper, 1985.

Borges de Macedo, J. et al. (1986), *A Adesao de Portugal a CEE*, Lisbon, Sociedad de Geografia de Lisboa.

Bourrinet, J. (ed.) (1987), *Les Relations Communauté Européenne Etats-Unis*, Paris, Economica.

Brugmans, H. et al. (1973), *The External Economic Policy of the Enlarged Community*, Bruges, De Tempel.

Bulletin of the European Communities, various numbers.

Bulletin of the European Communities (1986), *Single European Act* Supplement 2/86.

Burrows, B. and Edwards, G. (1982), *The Defense of Western Europe*, London, Butterworths.

Cahen, A. (1988), "Consequences of the EC Enlargements for Political Cooperation," *The Jerusalem Journal of International Relations*, Vol. 10, No. 3, September, pp. 1–10.

Clarck, R. P., and Haltzel, M. H. (1987), *Spain in the 1980s: The Democratic Transition and a New International Role*, Cambridge, Mass., Ballinger.

Coffey, P. and Wionczek, M. (eds.) (1987), *The EEC and Mexico*, Dordrecht, Martinus Nijhoff.

Commission of the European Communities (1983), *The European Community and Latin America*, Europe Information, No. 68/83, June.

Commission of the European Communities (1984), COM 107, final.

Commission of the European Communities (1986), *The Tourism Industry and the Tourism Policies of the Twelve Member States of the Community*, November, Doc. VII/473/86–EN.

Commission of the European Communities (1986), COM 720, December 2.

Commission of the European Communities (1986), COM 603, December 3.

Commission of the European Communities (1986), COM (86) 32, final, February 5.

Confederación Española de Organizaciones Empresariales (1987), *Primer Año. Balance de la Integración de España*, Madrid.

Council of the European Communities (1985), *Instruments Concerning the Accession of the Kingdom of Spain and the Portuguese Republic to the European Communities*, Vols. I—III.

Descallar, J., Cuestiones de interés permanente para España en el área mediterránea, Madrid, Centro Superior de Estudios de la Defensa Nacional, no date.

Donges, J. et al. (1982), *The Second Enlargement of the European Community*, Tübingen, Mohr.

Donges, J. and Schatz, K. W. (1985), *Portugal and Spain Entering the Common Market. Their Industrial Competitiveness Revisited*, Kiel Working Paper No. 233, Institut für Weltwirtschaft.

Dravet, J. F. (1986), *La Mediterranée, nouvelle frontière pour l'Europe des Douze ?*, Paris, Karthala.

Durán, E. (1985), *European Interests in Latin America*, London, Royal Institute for International Affairs, Chatham House Papers, No. 28.

Eckstein, A. M. (1985), "'Retrouvailles' timides entre les 'presque douze' et l'Amérique Latine," *Revue du Marché Commun*, No. 286, April, pp. 197–199.

El Independiente, various numbers.

El País, various numbers.

El País Internacional, various numbers.

Erdmann-Keefer, V., "The Corn War. Farm Interests in a Transatlantic Context," paper presented at the Sixth International Conference of Europeanists, Washington, D.C., November 1, 1987.

Estrella, R. (1987), "Europa y América Latina: La cooperación al desarrollo," *Leviatán*, No. 27, Spring, pp. 101–103.

Eurostat (1985), *Analysis of EC-Latin America Trade*, Luxembourg, Office des publications officielles des Communautés européennes.

Extebank, Boletín de Información Económica, various numbers.

Feld, W. (ed.) (1980), *Western Europe's Global Reach, Regional Cooperation and Worldwide Aspirations*, New York, Pergamon.

Fisas, V. (1987), *Paz en el Mediterráneo*, Barcelona, Lerna.

Flores, E. (1987), "Europa y América Latina, el desafío de la cooperación," *Leviatán*, No. 27, Spring, pp. 93–102.

Fuentes, J. (1986), "España y la seguridad internacional," *Revista de Estudios Internacionales*, Vol. 7, No. 4, October–December, pp. 1089–1105.

Garrigues Walker, A. (1985), *La vuelta a Europa*, Barcelona, Promociones Publicaciones Universitarias.

GATT, "Groupe de travail de l'adhesion du Portugal et de l'Espagne aux Communautés européennes," Doc. Spec. (86) 46, September 24, 1986.

Gil, F. G. and Tulchin J. S. (1988), *Spain's Entry into NATO*, Boulder, Lynne Rienner.

Ginsberg, R. (1983), "The European Community and the Mediterranean," in Lodge, J., *Institutions and Policies of the European Community*, pp. 154–167.

Glenn Mower, Jr., A. (1982), *The European Community and Latin America. A Case Study in Global Role Expansion*, Westport, Greenwood Press.

Granda Alva, G. and García J. L. (1984), "La cooperación para el desarrollo de las Comunidades Europeas y sus relaciones con América Latina: Un reto para España," *Estudios Internacionales*, Vol. 5, No.3, April–June, pp. 443–458.

Granell, F. (1984), Las relaciones económicas entre Europa y América Latina ante la ampliación de la CEE, unpublished paper.

Granell, F. (1986), *Política comercial y comercio exterior de España*, Barcelona, Orbis.

Granell, F. (1988), "La acción española de cooperación al desarollo," *Política Exterior*, Vol. 2, No. 6, Spring, pp. 257–274.

Grugel, J. (1987), "Spain's Socialist Government and Central American Dilemmas," *International Affairs*, Vol. 63, No. 4, Autumn, pp. 603–615.

Grupo Socialista del Parlamento Europeo (1987), *España-Europa: Trabajo Común, Los socialistas en el Parlamento Europeo*, Madrid.

Harvey D. R., and Thomson, K. J. (1985), "Costs, Benefits and the Future of the Common Agricultural Policy," *Journal of Common Market Studies*, Vol. 24, No. 1, September, pp. 1–20.

Hine, R. (1985), *The Political Economy of European Trade*, Sussex, Wheatsheaf.

Holmes, P. (1983), "Spain and the EEC," in Bell, D., (ed.), *Democratic Politics in Spain*, London, Francis Pinter, pp. 165–179.

Institut d'Etudes Européennes (1979), *L'Espagne et les Communautés européennes*, Bruxelles, Editions de l'Université de Bruxelles.

Institut d'Etudes Européennes (1981), *La Communauté Européenne et l'Amérique Latine*, Bruxelles, Editions de l'Université de Bruxelles.

International Herald Tribune, various numbers.

Ioakimidis, P. C., "Community Financial Flows to Mediterranean Countries," International Symposium on "Challenges to Mediterranean Cooperation and Security in the late 80s," Spetsae Island, Greece, May 28–31, 1987.

Josling, T. and Pearson, S. (1981), "Future developments in the Common Agricultural Policy of the European Community." Report submitted to the U.S. Department of Agriculture, Stanford, California.

Lafaye, J. J. (1984), "Entretien avec Fernando Morán: La nouvelle Espagne," *Politique Internationale*, No. 22, Winter, pp. 9–25.

Le Courrier, various numbers.

Lopez García, B. (1987), "Marruecos y el Maghreb en la política española," *Razón y Fe*, No. 1065, July–August, pp. 709–723.

Lorca, A. et al. (1984), *Un punto de vista español del área mediterránea como zona de interés prioritario*, Madrid, Instituto de Economía Aplicada, September.

Lorca, A., "El retorno de España al Mediterráneo," paper presented at the International Workshop on "The Enlarged EEC and the Mediterranean," Jerusalem, April 27–30, 1987.

Luciani, G. (ed.) (1984), *The Mediterranean Region*, London, Croom Helm.

Marquez, V. (1985), *Cien españoles y la OTAN*, Barcelona, Plaza y Janes.

McQueen, M., and Read, R. (1986), "Prospects for the Exports of the ACP Countries in a Community of Twelve," University of Reading Discussion Papers in European and International Social Science Research, No. 13, July.

Mediterranée-Sud, Selection d'articles de la presse, Direction Générale de l'Information, Communication et Culture, Commission of the European Communities, various numbers.

Melero, A. and Unamuno, J., "El desplazamiento del baricentro comercial de la CEE desde el Norte hacia el Sur, después de la Segunda Ampliación. Un punto de vista español," paper presented at the International Workshop on "The Enlarged EEC and the Mediterranean," Jerusalem, April 27–30, 1987.

Miguez, A. (1986), "Diplomatie espagnole: Le changement dans la continuité," *Politique internationale*, No. 30, Winter, pp. 335–343.

Minerbi, S. I. (1988), "Europe and the Middle East: An Israeli Perspective," *Jerusalem Journal of International Relations*, Vol. 10, No. 3, September, pp. 118–128.

Minet, G. et al. (1981), *Spain, Greece and Community Politics*, Brighton, Sussex European Papers, No. 11.

Ministerio Dos Negocios Estrangeiros (1986), *Portugal Nas Comunidades Europeias, Primero Ano.*

Morán, F. (1980), *Una Política Exterior para España*, Barcelona, Planeta.

Musto, S. (1983), "The European Community in Search of a New Mediterranean Policy: A Chance for a More Symmetrical Interdependence?," in Pinkele, C., and Pollis, A. (eds.), *The Contemporary Mediterranean World*, New York, Praeger, pp. 151–174.

Musto, S., "The Mediterranean Regions of an Enlarged EEC and the Community's Global Mediterranean Policy," paper presented at the IV General Conference of EADI, Madrid, 1984.

Musto, S. (1984), "La política mediterránea de la CEE: Piedra de toque de la capacidad de acción europea," *Revista de Instituciones Europeas*, Vol. 11, No. 1, January–April, pp. 9–32.

Musto, S., Spanien nach dem EG-Beitritt, unpublished paper, December 1985.

Musto, S. (1988), "The Common Agricultural Policy and the Mediterranean," *The Jerusalem Journal of International Relations*, Vol. 10, No. 3, September, pp. 55–84.

Nigoul, C., and Torelli, M. (1987), *Menaces en Mediterranée*, Paris, Fondation pour les Etudes de Defense Nationale.

Observatoire Stratégique Mediterranéen (1987), *O.T.A.N.: Flanc Nord-Flanc Sud. Les Perceptions de la Menace*, Nice, L'Europe en Formation,Cahiers No. 2.

Oldekop, D. (1981), "Alternatives for the Relations between Europe and Latin America in the Light of the Enlargement of the Communities," in Institut d'Etudes Européennes, *La Communauté Européenne et l'Amérique Latine*, Bruxelles, Editions de l'Université de Bruxelles, pp. 133–143.

Ortega, A. (1986), *El purgatorio de la OTAN*, Madrid, Ediciones El País.

Papeles de Economía Española, October 1985.

Pelkmans, J. (1984), *Market Integration in the European Community*, The Hague, Martinus Nijhoff.

Pelkmans, J. (ed.) (1985), *Can the CAP Be Reformed?*, Maastricht, European Institute of Public Administration.

Piñol, J. (1982), "España y Latinoamérica. El periodo Suárez (1976–80)," *Afers Internacionals*, No. 1, Spring, pp. 9–39.

Política Exterior (1987), Vol. I, No. 1, Winter.

Política Exterior (1987), Vol. I, No. 2, Spring.

Pollack, B. (1987), *The Paradox of Spanish Foreign Policy*, London, Pinter.

Pomfret, R. (1986), *Mediterranean Policy of the European Community. A*

Study of Discrimination in Trade, London, Macmillan (for the Trade Policy Research Centre).

Praet, P. (1988), "The Change of the Baricenter of the EEC from a New Hanseatic League to a Southern-Oriented Community: A View from the Center," *The Jerusalem Journal of International Relations*, Vol. 10, No. 3, September, pp. 33–54.

Preston, P., and Smyth, P. (1984), *Spain, the EEC and NATO*, Royal Institute of International Affairs, Chatham House Papers, No. 22.

Pridham, G. (ed.) (1984), *The New Mediterranean Democracies. Regime Transition in Spain, Greece and Portugal*, London, Frank Cass.

PSOE (1985), *Una política de paz y seguridad para España*, Madrid, December.

PSOE (1986), *Por buen camino*, Programa 1986/1990,: Madrid.

Regelsberger, E. (1985), "From Ten to Twelve: A New Dimension for the EPC," *International Spectator*, July–December, No. 3/4, pp. 33–44.

Reig, E. (1984), *Spain's Economic Problems and Policies, Prospects before EEC Membership*, University of Reading, Discussion Papers in European and International Science Research, No. 2, October.

Riera, L., "España, país comunitario: El desarme arancelario," unpublished paper, June 1985.

Rosenthal, G. (1982), *The Mediterranean Basin: Its political economy and Changing International Relations*, London, Butterworths.

Rummel, R., "Concentric Integration? The Impact of Greek, Spanish and Portuguese Membership on Western Europe as a Foreign Policy Actor," paper presented at the Sixth International Conference of Europeanists, Washington, D.C., November 1987.

Ruperez, J. (1986), *España en la OTAN*, Barcelona, Plaza y Janes.

Salgado Albor, J. (1987), España en el mundo actual, *Boletín de Información*, No. 199–VIII, CESEDEN, March.

Sampson, G. and Yeats, A. (1977), "An Evaluation of the Common Agricultural Policy as a Barrier Facing Agricultural Exports to the European Community," *American Journal of Agricultural Economics*, February, pp. 99–106.

Sampson, G. and Snape R. (1980), "Effects of the EEC's Variable Import Levies," *Journal of Political Economy*, Vol. 88, No. 5, October, pp. 1026–1040.

Sanchez-Gijón, A. (1983), *Spain and International Security Issues: the NATO Relationship*, Boston, Tufts University, Murrow Reports, March.

Santos, A. (1985), "Le bousculement vers le Sud de la politique de defense de l'Espagne," *Afers Internacionals*, Autumn–Winter, No. 7.

Sarasqueta, A. (1985), *Después de Franco, la OTAN*, Barcelona, Plaza y Janes.

Sawyer, C. (1984), "The Effects of the Second Enlargement of the EC on US Exports to Europe," *Weltwirtschaftliches Archiv*, Vol. 120, No. 3, pp. 572–578.

Schneider, J.W. (ed.) (1980), *From Nine to Twelve: Europe's Destiny?*, Alphen aan den Rijn, Sijthoff and Noordhoff.

Sebastian, L. De, "España, es realmente puente entre Europa y América Latina?," *Muga*, September 1985, pp. 54–67.

Secretaría de Estado para las Comunidades Europeas (1987), *Balance del primer año de la adhesión de España a la C.E.E.*, Madrid, Oficina de Información Diplomática.

Shafir, D. (1982), *The Strategic Significance of the Mediterranean Sea*, Tel Aviv, Tel Aviv University, Center for Strategic Studies, Paper No. 15, April.

Sicherman, H. (1985), "Europe's Role in the Middle East: Illusions and Realities," Orbis, Winter, pp. 803–828.

Siqueira Freire, A. de (1986), *A Adesao de Portugal as Comunidades Europeias e o Mediterraneo*, Lisbon, Instituto de Estudios Estrategicos e Internacionais.

Siqueira Freire, A. de (1983), "Le Portugal, la Mediterranée et l'Atlantique," *Naçao e Defesa*, January–March, No. 33, pp. 3–19.

Spain and the United States (1983), Boston, Fletcher School of Law and Diplomacy.

Stiftung Wissenschaft und Politik (1980), *Konsequenzen der Süderweiterung für die Stellung der EG im Nord-Süd Kontext*, Eggenberg, Ebenhausen.

Tamames, R. (1986), *Guía del Mercado Común Europeo, España en la Europa de los Doce*, Madrid, Alianza Editorial.

Telex Mediterranée, various numbers.

The Economist, various numbers.

Tovias, A. (1977), *Tariff Preferences in Mediterranean Diplomacy*, London, Macmillan (for the Trade Policy Research Centre).

Tovias, A. (1979), *EEC Enlargement: The Southern Neighbours*, Brighton, Sussex European Papers No. 5.

Tovias, A. (1984), "The Effects of the Second Enlargement of the European Community upon Israel's Economy," in Gutmann, E. (ed.), *Israel and the Second Enlargement of the European Community: Political and Economic Aspects*, Jerusalem, The Hebrew University.

Tovias, A. (1988), "The Impact of the Southern Enlargement of the European Community on Its System of Foreign Relations," *The Jerusalem Journal of International Relations*, Vol. 10, No. 3, September, pp. 11–32.

Tovias, A. (1989), "Iberian Countries, Iberoamerica and the European Community," *The World Economy*, Vol. 12, No. 1, March, pp. 105–115.

Treverton, G. (1986), "Spain: Domestic Politics and Security Policy," *Adelphi Papers*, No. 204, Spring.

Viñas, A. (1984), Spain, "The United States and NATO," in Abel, C., and Torrents N. (eds.), *Spain's Conditional Democracy*, London, Croom Helm.

Wallace, W., and Herreman, I. (1978), *A Community of Twelve? The Impact of Further Enlargement of the European Communities*, Bruges, De Tempel.

Wessels, W., "European Political Cooperation and the European Union: Brake or Engine for Future Integration? Some Remarks," unpublished paper, 1985.

Weston, A., et al. (1980), *The EEC's Generalized System of Preferences*, London, Overseas Development Institute.

"What Role for Spain in NATO?" (1982), *Atlantic Community Quarterly*, Vol. 20, No. 2, Summer, pp. 139–142.

Williams, A. (ed.) (1984), *Southern Europe Transformed, Political and*

Economic Change in Greece, Italy, Portugal and Spain, London, Harper and Row.

Yañez, L. (1984), "Recuperación democrática y relaciones con Ibero-américa," *Afers Internacionals*, No. 3, Spring, pp. 39–46.

Yannopoulos, G. (1983), "The Impact of the Common Agricultural Policy on Developing Countries following the Enlargement of the European Community," *Development Policy Review*, Vol. 1, pp. 197–218.

Yannopoulos, G. (1984), "Prospects for the Manufacturing Exports of the Non-Candidate Mediterranean Countries in a Community of Twelve," *World Development*, Vol. 12, No. 11/12, pp. 1087–1094.

Yannopoulos, G. (1985), "Integration and Convergence, Lessons from Greece's Experience in the European Community," *Intereconomics*, March–April, Vol. 20, No. 20, pp. 93–96.

Yannopoulos, G. (1985), "The European Community's Common External Commercial Policy: Internal Contradictions and Institutional Weaknesses," *Journal of World Trade Law*, Vol. 19, No. 5, pp. 451–465.

Yannopoulos, G. (1987), *The Trade Interests of the United States and the Enlargement of the EC*, University of Reading, Discussion Papers in European and International Social Science Research, No. 17, March.

Yannopoulos, G. (1987), "The Challenge of the Southern Enlargement of the European Community," *Il Politico*, No. 3, pp. 427–436.

Yannopoulos,G. (1988), *Customs Unions and Trade Conflicts*, London, Routledge.

Interviews

In Spain

Mr. Ferrer, Ministry of Foreign Affairs

Mr. Granell, University of Barcelona and Barcelona's Chamber of Commerce; since 1989 director general of the Commission of the EC, formerly Director of Trade Promotion at the Catalan Autonomic Government

Mr. Herrero, PSOE, European desk

Mr. Lorca, Instituto de Economia y Geografia Aplicadas, Consejo Superior de Investigaciones Cientificas

Mr. Moratines, Ministry of Foreign Affairs

Mr. Mogo, PSOE, Latin American desk

Mr. Muns, deputy in the European Parliament

Mr. Yañez, Secretary of State for International Cooperation and Iberoamerica

In Portugal

Mr. Alabart, Spain's Commercial Office in Portugal

Mr. Ferran, Spanish Ambassador to Portugal

Mr. Magalhaes, Institute of Strategic Studies

Mr. Sarsfield Cabral, Ministry of Foreign Affairs

Mr. Siqueira Freire, former ambassador, Institute of Strategic Studies

Mr. Vasconcelos, Institute of Strategic Studies

At the EC Commission

Mr. Bang-Hansen
Mr. Benavides
Mr. Durrieux
Mrs. Lastenouse
Mr. Leigh
Mr. Mansito
Mr. Renier
Mr. Russell
Mr. Schwed
Mr. Siotis
Mr. Van Ringelstein
Mr. Viñas
Mr. Wyatt

Index

Accession Treaty. *See* Treaty of Accession

Africa, relations with Portugal, 87-89, 90-91, 118n; relations with Spain, 87, 88, 89-90

Agriculture, land area, 15; leading exporter, 94

air transport, deregulation of, 26

Algeria, relations with Spain, 73, 74

Angola, 88

Arab world, dialogue with, 84-85, 118n

Asia, relations with Portugal, 94

Atlantic Alliance, 16

Balearic Islands, 71, 72

Baron, Enrique, 45, 114n

Calvo-Sotelo, Leopoldo, 46

Canary Islands, 71, 72, 78-79, 109

CAP. *See* Common Agricultural Policy

Castiella, Fernando María, 72

Caudillo, 46

Central American Bank for Economic Integration, 69

Ceuta, 71,72

Cheysson Document, 65

China, relations with Portugal, 94

Club of Paris, 70

Coastal length of European Community, 15-16

Commission. *See* European Community Commission

Common Agricultural Policy, 1, 42-43, 50; effects on Spain, 77-78; and Mediterranean agricultural products, 115n; reform of, 31-32; and relations with United States, 96-97

Common Commercial Policy, 41, 95

Common External Tariff, 77

Community of the Nine, 4, 6

Community of the Six, 4, 6

Community of the Ten, 6, 106; international air links, 54-56, 56 (table); oil and gas import dependence, 23-26, 24 (table), 26 (table); outside perception of, 32-34; outside sources of imports, 21; outside trade relations, 21, 22-23; and Portugal, 19, 21; and Spain, 17, 21; trade vulnerability, 24

Cooperation Agreement with Yugoslavia, 114n

Council of Ministers, 69; power of president of, 38; Spanish attitude toward presidency of, 38-39

Court of Justice; independence from national governments, 37

Customs Union, 1, 26

Cyprus; and European Community, 6

EC Commission. *See* European Community Commission

Economic changes on individual EC members, effect of, 105

EDF. *See* European Development Fund

EFTA. *See* European Free Trade Association

Egypt, relations with Spain, 73, 117n

EIB. *See* European Investment Bank

EMS. *See* European Monetary System

English-speaking members of

European Community, 16
EP. *See* European Parliament
EPC. *See* European Political Cooperation
European Community Commission, 37-38, 39
European Development Fund, 44
European Free Trade Association, 4, 5; Portuguese Industrial Development Fund, 93; relations with Spain, 91-93
European Investment Bank, 67
European Monetary System, 1
European Parliament, 1; change in political structure, 29-32, 32 (table); European-wide elections, 31; and foreign debt, 31; and Generalized System of Preferences, 31; Iberian voting power in, 37; ideological dilution of national voting power, 37; Socialist representation, 31
European Political Cooperation, 1, 40
Euzkadi Ta Azkatasuna, 73
Export destinations, 17, 18 (table), 19
External trade policy, 3-6

FAD. *See* Spain, Development Aid Fund
Falklands War (1982), 64
Fish export, 95
Fisheries policy, 39, 95; in Portugal, 98; and relations with United States, 98-100; in Spain, 98
Foreign aid. *See* European Development Fund, Official Development Assistance
Foreign relations; indexes of sensitivity toward other areas, 54
France; influence in European Community Commission, 39; position in European Community, 114n; relations with Spain, 117n
Franco, Francisco, 72, 76; foreign policy, 46

GATT. *See* General Agreement on Tariffs and Trade
General Agreement on Tariffs and Trade, 2, 3, 4, 95, 110; Iberian attitude toward, 41; and Portu-

guese agricultural protectionism, 42
General Treaty on Central American Economic Integration and Panama, 66
Generalized System of Preferences, 4, 65, 68; and European Parliament, 31; Iberian attitude toward, 41
Germany, influence in European Community Commission, 39
Global Mediterranean Policy, 5
GMP. *See* Global Mediterranean Policy
GNP. *See* Gross national product
Gonzalez, Felipe, 50, 63, 75, 84
Great Britain; influence in European Community, 39, 40; relations with Commonwealth, 64.
Greece; entry into European Community; 6; influence in European Community, 40-41; per capita GNP compared with other nations, 67, 68 (table)
Grenada; Spanish reaction to U.S. invasion of, 99
Gross national product, 16
GSP. *See* Generalized System of Preferences
Guerra, Alfonso, 83

Hassan II, King of Morocco, 83, 86
High-technology products, policy on, 97-98

Iberian countries; and adjustment process, 11-12; agricultural trade, 7-8; attitudes toward foreign aid, 43-46; and Eastern Mediterranean countries, 8, 9, 10; effect on developing relations with Africa, 89-91; effect on external trade relations, 106-107; effect on Mediterranean Policy, 76-81, 108; effect on relations with Morocco, 109; effect on relations with United States, 94-98; effect on trade policy, 41-43; and European Community, 7-10, 12-13, 15-16, 48-51, 81-84, 106, 116n, 118n; industrial trade, 8; opposition to "reverse trade diversion," 106; and protection-

ism, 12; share in decisionmaking institutions, 38 (table); tariff adjustments, 7; trade relations, 8-10. *See also* Portugal, Spain
Import sources, 20 (table)
Institutional reform, 10
Integrated Mediterranean Programs, 43, 67
Integration process, 11
Internal Market, 10, 41
International air links, 54-56, 56 (table)
International Monetary Fund, 70
Islam, relations with Spain, 72-73
Israel, relations with Spain, 76, 99

Joint Cooperation Committee (European Community and Latin America), 66
Joint Declaration of Intent, 64, 65
Juan Carlos, King of Spain, 75

Kissinger, Henry, 99

Latin America; policy, 39, 70; relations with European Community, 65, 66; relations with Portugal, 63, 66; relations with Spain, 60-66, 67-70, 109-110
Libya, relations with Spain, 73, 117n
Lomé Convention, 5, 68, 88, 102, 107, 110
Luxembourg compromise, 39

Macao, 94
Malta; and European Community, 6
Mauritania, relations with Spain, 73
Mediterranean lobby, 36, 37 (table), 110-111
Mediterranean policy, 107; development of, 78-79
Mediterranean share in decisionmaking institutions, 38 (table)
Melilla, 71, 72
MFA. *See* Multi-Fibre Arrangement
Mitterrand, François, 83-84
Morán, Fernando, 47
Morocco; potential membership in European Community, 86-87 ; relations with Portugal, 74-75, 109, 118n; relations with Spain, 73, 74, 80-81, 109; tourism, 71

Multi-Fibre Arrangement, 41
Multiple trade discrimination policy, 43

NATO. *See* North Atlantic Treaty Organization
Newly Industrializing Countries, 68
NIC. *See* Newly Industrializing Countries
Northern Africa, relations with Spain, 71-73, 117n
North Atlantic Treaty Organization, 16
Norway, 114n

ODA. *See* Official Development Assistance
OECD. *See* Organization for Economic Cooperation and Development
Official Development Assistance; European Community members, 44 (table); in nonmember Mediterranean states, 82; Ireland, 43-44; Italy, 43-44; Portugal, 46; Spain, 43-45, 45 (table)
Oil dependency, 16
Ordoñez, Fernandez, 79
Organization for Economic Cooperation and Development, 4

Peres, Shimon; call for Middle Eastern "Marshall Plan," 82
Política Exterior, 47
Portugal; and Africa, 87-89, 90-91, 118n; and agricultural protectionism, 42; and Angola, 88; and Asia, 94; and Brazil, 62; and Canary Islands, 109; and China, 94; and Community of the Ten, 19, 21; effect on European Community tourism industry, 26-29; emigration, 59, 60; entry into European Community, 1; and European Free Trade Association countries, 93; European Parliament, 31; export destinations, 17, 93; fishery policies, 98; foreign relations, 48; import sources, 19; influence in European Community, 63, 66, 115n; influence on European Communi-

ty's Mediterranean policy, 79-81; international air links, 56 (table); and Latin America, 63, 66; and Macao, 94; and Mediterranean countries, 75, 76; and Morocco, 74-75, 109, 118n; national identity, 100-101; Official Development Assistance, 46, 47 (table); per capita GNP, 67, 68 (table); share of European Community GNP, 36, 37 (table); share of European Community population, 36, 37 (table); share in decisionmaking institutions, 38 (table); and South Africa, 88, 90-91; and Spain, 17, 21, 119n; tourism, 54, 55 (table); trade policy, 41; trade relations, 21; and Turkey, 109. *See also* Iberian countries
Portuguese Industrial Development Fund, 93
Protectionism, 11

SEA. *See* Single European Act
Second Enlargement, 6
Silva, Cavaco, 50
Single European Act, 1, 10, 39, 49, 95
Socialist party, 31, 44-45, 66
South Africa, relations with Portugal, 88, 90-91
Southern Enlargement, effects on nonmember countries, 2-3
Southern lobby, 50
Spain; and Africa, 87, 88, 89-90; agricultural exports, 77; agricultural protectionism, 42-43; and Algeria, 73, 74; and Arabs, 84-85; and Asia, 93-94; and Canary Islands, 78-79, 109; and Community of the Ten, 17, 21; and Council of Ministers, 38-39, 69; Development Aid Fund, 44; and Egypt, 73, 117n; emigration, 58-60, 59 (table); energy dependence, 71; and European Community Commission, 37-38, 39; and European Free Trade Association, 91-93; and European Parliament, 31, 116n; export destinations, 17; fishery

policies, 98; foreign policy history, 46-47; and France, 117n; import sources, 19; influence on European Community's Mediterranean policy, 75-81; integration into European Community, 1, 48; international air links, 47, 56 (table); investments, 56-58, 58 (table), 61; and Islam, 72-73; isolationism, 47-48; and Israel, 76, 79; and Latin America, 60-66, 67-70, 109-110; and Libya, 73, 117n; and Mauritania, 73; Ministry of Foreign Affairs, 71, 74; and Morocco, 71, 73, 74, 80-81, 109; and NATO, 71, 72; and Northern Africa, 71-73, 117n; Official Development Assistance, 43-45, 45 (table); per capita GNP, 67, 68 (table); and Portugal, 17, 21, 119n; pro-Europeanism, 113n; share in decisionmaking institutions, 38 (table); share of European Community GNP, 36, 37 (table); share of European Community population, 36, 37 (table); Socialist party, 44-45, 66; and Southern lobby, 50; tariff adjustments, 77; tourism, 26-29, 54, 55 (table); trade deficit, 41-42; trade policy, 41; trade relations, 21, 118n; and Tunisia, 73; and Turkey, 109; and United States, 98-100, 119n; views on European Community's external economic relations, 100-103; voting patterns, 114n. *See also* Iberian countries

Tax-free shopping, 26
Third Enlargement (Spain and Portugal), 6-10
Third World, relations with European Community, 108, 109
Tindemans, Leo, 64
Tourism activities, 26-29, 95
Trade; dependence of outside world, 16-23, 29, 30 (table); preferred partners, 107; regional approach to, 4-5; relations with Eastern Mediterranean countries, 5-6

Treaty of Accession, 8, 9, 64-65, 77; and Portuguese agricultural protectionism, 42
Treaty of Rome, 1, 26
Tunisia, relations with Spain, 73
Turkey; and European Community, 6; potential membership in European Community, 85-86; relations with Portugal, 109; relations with Spain, 109

United Nations Conference on Trade and Development, 95
United States, as trading power, 94-96; relations with Latin America, 110
Uruguay Round of Multilateral Trade Negotiations, 98

Valcarcel, Daniel, 47
Veto power, 39

World Bank, 70

Yañez, Luis, 45, 88
Yom Kippur War, 76
Yugoslavia; Cooperation Agreement with European Community, 114n

About the Book and the Author

Providing a wealth of primary source data on the European Community after the accession of Spain and Portugal, Alfred Tovias assesses the changes—demographic, economic, and cultural—that have occurred thus far as a result of the third enlargement and posits that a further result will be the development of new EC foreign policies. Tovias traces the evolving character of the EC and, given the newest members' foreign policy affinities—and antipathies—explores the impact of Spain and Portugal on the Community's foreign economic policymaking. He also discusses present and likely future policies toward specific geographic regions. Although he sees an enhanced foreign policy profile for the enlarged EC, his data do not support the notion of a significant change in EC-Latin American relations, nor of a "Mediterranean lobby."

Alfred Tovias is senior lecturer in international relations at the Hebrew University of Jerusalem. He also lectures regularly at the Europa Institute of the University of Amsterdam. He is author of *Tariff Preferences in Mediterranean Diplomacy* and coauthor of *The Economics of Peace-making.*